INDIA:
A WOUNDED
CIVILIZATION

INDIA:
A WOUNDED
CIVILIZATION

V. S. Naipaul

VINTAGE BOOKS
A Division of Random House
New York

FIRST VINTAGE BOOKS EDITION, January 1978

Copyright © 1976, 1977 by V. S. Naipaul
All rights reserved under International and Pan-American
Copyright Conventions. Published in the United States by
Random House, Inc., New York, and simultaneously in
Canada by Random House of Canada Limited, Toronto.
Originally published by Alfred A. Knopf, Inc., in 1977.
Most of this book was first published in *The New York
Review of Books*.

Library of Congress Cataloging in Publication Data

Naipaul, Vidiadhar Surajprasad.
  India: a wounded civilization.

  1. India—Collected Works. I. Title.
DS407.N26 1978   954   77-76571
ISBN 0-394-72463-1

Manufactured in the United States of America

Contents

Foreword   vii

PART ONE: A WOUNDED CIVILIZATION

1. An Old Equilibrium   3

2. The Shattering World   31

PART TWO: A NEW CLAIM ON THE LAND

3. The Skyscrapers and the Chawls   55

4. The House of Grain   73

PART THREE: NOT IDEAS, BUT OBSESSIONS

5. A Defect of Vision   101

6. Synthesis and Mimicry   124

7. Paradise Lost   145

8. Renaissance or Continuity?   166

Foreword

The lights of Bombay airport showed that it had been raining; and the airplane, as it taxied in, an hour or two after midnight, blew the monsoon puddles over the concrete. This was in mid-August; and officially (though this monsoon was to be prolonged) the monsoon still had two weeks to go. In the small, damp terminal building there were passengers from an earlier flight, by Gulf Air. The Gulf was the Persian Gulf, with the oil states. And among the passengers were Indian businessmen in suits, awaiting especially careful search by the customs men; some Japanese; a few Arabs in the desert costumes which now, when seen in airports and foreign cities, are like the white gowns of a new and suddenly universal priesthood of pure money; and two turbaned and sunburnt Sikhs, artisans, returning to India after their work in an oil state, with cardboard suitcases and similar new shoes in yellow suede.

There is a new kind of coming and going in the world these days. Arabia, lucky again, has spread beyond its deserts. And India is again at the periphery of this new Arabian world, as much as it had been in the eighth cen-

tury, when the new religion of Islam spread in all directions
and the Arabs—led, it is said, by a seventeen-year-old boy—
overran the Indian kingdom of Sind. That was only an
episode, the historians say. But Sind is not a part of India
today; India has shrunk since that Arab incursion. No
civilization was so little equipped to cope with the outside
world; no country was so easily raided and plundered, and
learned so little from its disasters. Five hundred years after
the Arab conquest of Sind, Moslem rule was established in
Delhi as the rule of foreigners, people apart; and foreign
rule—Moslem for the first five hundred years, British for
the last 150—ended in Delhi only in 1947.

Indian history telescopes easily; and in India this time,
in a northern city, I was to meet a young man, a civil
servant, who said his Arab ancestors had come to India
eight centuries before, during the great Islamic push of the
twelfth century. When I asked where he lived, he said,
"My family has been living in Delhi for five hundred years."
And what in Europe would have sounded like boasting
wasn't boasting in India. The family was a modest one, had
always been modest, their surname, Qureshi, indicating
the religious functions they had performed throughout the
centuries. The entry of a member of the family into the
Administrative Service was a break with the static past, a
step up after eight hundred years. The young man compared
his family with those of the Moslem masons and stone-
cutters, descendants of the builders of the Mughal palaces
and mosques, who in Delhi still sat around Shah Jehan's
great mosque, the Jama Masjid, craftsmen as needy and
as ragged as their ancestors had been, each man displaying
the tools of the craft he had inherited, waiting to be hired,
ready to build anybody a new Delhi.

India in the late twentieth century still seems so much itself, so rooted in its own civilization, it takes time to understand that its independence has meant more than the going away of the British; that the India to which Independence came was a land of far older defeat; that the purely Indian past died a long time ago. And already, with the Emergency, it is necessary to fight against the chilling sense of a new Indian dissolution.

India is for me a difficult country. It isn't my home and cannot be my home; and yet I cannot reject it or be indifferent to it; I cannot travel only for the sights. I am at once too close and too far. My ancestors migrated from the Gangetic plain a hundred years ago; and the Indian community they and others established in Trinidad, on the other side of the world, the community in which I grew up, was more homogeneous than the Indian community Gandhi met in South Africa in 1893, and more isolated from India.

India, which I visited for the first time in 1962, turned out to be a very strange land. A hundred years had been enough to wash me clean of many Indian religious attitudes; and without these attitudes the distress of India was —and is—almost insupportable. It has taken me much time to come to terms with the strangeness of India, to define what separates me from the country; and to understand how far the "Indian" attitudes of someone like myself, a member of a small and remote community in the New World, have diverged from the attitudes of people to whom India is still whole.

An inquiry about India—even an inquiry about the

Emergency—has quickly to go beyond the political. It has to be an inquiry about Indian attitudes; it has to be an inquiry about the civilization itself, as it is. And though in India I am a stranger, the starting point of this inquiry—more than might appear in these pages—has been myself. Because in myself, like the split-second images of infancy which some of us carry, there survive, from the family rituals that lasted into my childhood, phantasmal memories of old India which for me outline a whole vanished world.

I know, for instance, the beauty of sacrifice, so important to the Aryans. Sacrifice turned the cooking of food into a ritual: the first cooked thing—usually a small round of unleavened bread, a miniature, especially made—was always for the fire, the god. This was possible only with an open fireplace; to have to give up the custom—if I attempt now to expand on what to a child was only a passing sense of wrongness—was to abjure a link with the earth and the antiquity of the earth, the beginning of things. The morning rituals before breakfast, the evening ritual before the lighting of the lamps: these went, one by one, links with a religion that was also like a sense of the past, so that awe in the presence of the earth and the universe was something that had to be rediscovered later, by other means.

The customs of my childhood were sometimes mysterious. I didn't know it at the time, but the smooth pebbles in the shrine in my grandmother's house, pebbles brought by my grandfather all the way from India with his other household gods, were phallic emblems: the pebbles, of stone, standing for the more blatant stone columns. And why was it necessary for a male hand to hold the knife with which a pumpkin was cut open? It seemed to me at one time—because of the appearance of a pumpkin halved downward—that there was some sexual element in the rite. The truth is more frightening, as I learned only recently, near the end of this book. The pumpkin, in Bengal and adjoining areas, is a vegetable substitute for a living sacrifice: the male hand was therefore necessary. In India I know I am a stranger; but increasingly I understand that my Indian memories, the memories of that India which lived on into my childhood in Trinidad, are like trapdoors into a bottomless past.

Part One

A WOUNDED CIVILIZATION

1

An Old Equilibrium

1

Sometimes old India, the old, eternal India many Indians
like to talk about, does seem just to go on. During the last
war some British soldiers, who were training in chemical
warfare, were stationed in the far south of the country,
near a thousand-year-old Hindu temple. The temple had
a pet crocodile. The soldiers, understandably, shot the crocodile. They also in some way—perhaps by their presence
alone—defiled the temple. Soon, however, the soldiers went
away and the British left India altogether. Now, more
than thirty years after that defilement, and in another
season of emergency, the temple has been renovated and
a new statue of the temple deity is being installed.

Until they are given life and invested with power, such
statues are only objects in an image-maker's yard, their
value depending on size, material, and the carver's skill.
Hindu idols or images come from the old world; they
embody difficult and sometimes sublime concepts, and they

have to be made according to certain rules. There can be no development now in Hindu iconography, though the images these days, under the influence of the Indian cinema and cinema posters, are less abstract than their ancient originals, and more humanly pretty and doll-like. They stand lifeless in every way in the image-maker's showroom. Granite and marble—and an occasional commissioned bust of someone like a local inspector of police, with perhaps a real spectacle frame over his blank marble eyes—suggest at first the graveyard, and a people in love with death. But this showroom is a kind of limbo, with each image awaiting the life and divinity that will come to it with purchase and devotion, each image already minutely flawed so that its divine life, when it comes, shall not be terrible and over-whelming.

Life, then, has to be given to the new image in the once defiled temple. A special effort has to be made. And the method being used is one of the most archaic in the world. It takes us back to the beginning of religion and human wonder. It is the method of the word: in the beginning was the word. A twelve-lettered *mantra* will be chanted and written fifty million times; and that is what—in this time of Emergency, with the constitution suspended, the press censored—five thousand volunteers are doing. When the job is completed, an inscribed gold plate will be placed below the new idol to attest to the creation of its divinity and the devotion of the volunteers. A thousand-year-old temple will live again: India, Hindu India, is eternal: conquests and defilements are but instants in time.

About two hundred miles away, still in the south, on a brown plateau of rock and gigantic boulders, are the ruins of the capital city of what was once the great Hindu kingdom of Vijayanagar. Vijayanagar—*vijaya*, victory, *nagar*, city—was established in the fourteenth century; it was conquered, and totally destroyed, by an alliance of Moslem principalities in 1565. The city was then one of the greatest in the world, its walls twenty-four miles around—foreign visitors have left accounts of its organization and magnificence—and the work of destruction took five months; some people say a year.

Today all the outer city is a peasant wilderness, with scattered remnants of stone or brick structures. Near the Tungabhadra River are the grander ruins: palaces and stables, a royal bath, a temple with clusters of musical stone columns that can still be played, a broken aqueduct, the leaning granite pillars of what must have been a bridge across the river. There is more beyond the river: a long and very wide avenue, still partly façaded, with a giant statue of the bull of Shiva at one end and at the other end a miracle: a temple that for some reason was spared destruction four hundred years ago, is still whole, and is still used for worship.

It is for this that the pilgrims come, to make offerings and to perform the rites of old magic. Some of the ruins of Vijayanagar have been declared national monuments by the Archaeological Department; but to the pilgrims—and they are more numerous than the tourists—Vijayanagar is not its terrible history or its present encompassing desolation. Such history as is known has been reduced to the legend of a mighty ruler, a kingdom founded with gold that showered from the sky, a kingdom so rich that pearls and rubies were sold in the market place like grain.

To the pilgrims Vijayanagar is its surviving temple. The surrounding destruction is like proof of the virtue of old magic; just as the fantasy of past splendor is accommodated

within an acceptance of present squalor. That once glorious
avenue—not a national monument, still permitted to live
—is a slum. Its surface, where unpaved, is a green-black
slurry of mud and excrement, through which the sandaled
pilgrims unheedingly pad to the food stalls and souvenir
shops, loud and gay with radios. And there are starved
squatters with their starved animals in the ruins, the broken
stone façades patched up with mud and rocks, the doorways
stripped of the sculptures which existed until recently. Life
goes on, the past continues. After conquest and destruction,
the past simply reasserts itself.

If Vijayanagar is now only its name and, as a kingdom,
is so little remembered (there are university students in
Bangalore, two hundred miles away, who haven't even
heard of it), it isn't only because it was so completely wiped
out, but also because it contributed so little; it was itself a
reassertion of the past. The kingdom was founded in 1336
by a local Hindu prince who, after defeat by the Moslems,
had been taken to Delhi, converted to Islam, and then
sent back to the south as a representative of the Moslem
power. There in the south, far from Delhi, the converted
prince had reestablished his independence and, unusually,
in defiance of Hindu caste rules, had declared himself a
Hindu again, a representative on earth of the local Hindu
god. In this unlikely way the great Hindu kingdom of the
south was founded.

It lasted two hundred years, but during that time it never
ceased to be embattled. It was committed from the start to
the preservation of a Hinduism that had already been violated, and culturally and artistically it preserved and repeated; it hardly innovated. Its bronze sculptures are like
those of five hundred years before; its architecture, even at

the time, and certainly to the surrounding Moslems, must
have seemed heavy and archaic. And its ruins today, in that
unfriendly landscape of rock and boulders of strange shapes,
look older than they are, like the ruins of a long-superseded
civilization.

The Hinduism Vijayanagar proclaimed had already
reached a dead end, and in some ways had decayed, as
popular Hinduism so easily decays, into barbarism. Vijayanagar had its slave markets, its temple prostitutes. It encouraged the holy practice of *suttee*, whereby a widow burned
herself on the funeral pyre of her husband, to achieve
virtue, to secure the honor of her husband's family, and to
cleanse that family of the sins of three generations. And
Vijayanagar dealt in human sacrifice. Once, when there was
some trouble with the construction of a big reservoir, the
great king of Vijayanagar, Krishna Deva Raya (1509–1529),
ordered the sacrifice of some prisoners.

In the sixteenth century Vijayanagar, really, was a kingdom awaiting conquest. But it was big and splendid; it
needed administrators, artists, craftsmen; and for the two
hundred years of its life it must have sustained all the
talent of the land and concentrated it in that capital. When
it was conquered and its capital systematically smashed,
more than buildings and temples would have been destroyed. Many men would have been killed; all the talent,
energy, and intellectual capacity of the kingdom would
have been extinguished for generations. The conquerors
themselves, by creating a desert, would have ensured, almost
invited, their own subsequent defeat by others: again and
again, for the next two hundred years, the land of that
dead kingdom was trampled down.

And today it still shows, the finality of that destruction

of Hindu Vijayanagar in 1565: in the acknowledged "back-wardness" of the region, which now seems without a history and which it is impossible to associate with past grandeur or even with great wars; in the squalor of the town of Hospet that has grown up not far from the ruins; in the unending nullity of the peasant-serf countryside.

Since Independence much money has been spent on the region. A dam has been built across the Tungabhadra River. There is an extensive irrigation scheme which incorporates the irrigation canals of the old kingdom (and these are still called Vijayanagar canals). A Vijayanagar steel plant is being planned; and a university is being built, to train men of the region for jobs in that steel plant and the sub-sidiary industries that are expected to come up. The emphasis is on training men of the region, local men. Because, in this land that was once a land of great builders, there is now a human deficiency. The state of which the region forms part is the one state in the Indian Union that encour-ages migrants from other states. It needs technicians, arti-sans; it needs men with simple skills; it needs even hotel waiters. All it has been left with is a peasantry that cannot comprehend the idea of change: like the squatters in the ruins outside the living Vijayanagar temple, slipping in and out of the decayed stone façades like brightly colored insects, screeching and unimportantly active on this after-noon of rain.

It was at Vijayanagar this time, in that wide temple avenue, which seemed less awesome than when I had first seen it thirteen years before, no longer speaking as directly as it did then of a fabulous past, that I began to wonder about the intellectual depletion that must have come to

India with the invasions and conquests of the last thousand years. What happened in Vijayanagar happened, in varying degrees, in other parts of the country. In the north, ruin lies on ruin: Moslem ruin on Hindu ruin, Moslem on Moslem. In the history books, in the accounts of wars and conquests and plunder, the intellectual depletion passes unnoticed, the lesser intellectual life of a country whose contributions to civilization were made in the remote past. India absorbs and outlasts its conquerors, Indians say. But at Vijayanagar, among the pilgrims, I wondered whether intellectually for a thousand years India hadn't always retreated before its conquerors and whether, in its periods of apparent revival, India hadn't only been making itself archaic again, intellectually smaller, always vulnerable.

In the British time, a period of bitter subjection which was yet for India a period of intellectual recruitment, Indian nationalism proclaimed the Indian past; and religion was inextricably mixed with political awakening. But independent India, with its five-year plans, its industrialization, its practice of democracy, has invested in change. There always was a contradiction between the archaism of national pride and the promise of the new; and the contradiction has at last cracked the civilization open.

The turbulence in India this time hasn't come from foreign invasion or conquest; it has been generated from within. India cannot respond in her old way, by a further retreat into archaism. Her borrowed institutions have worked like borrowed institutions; but archaic India can provide no substitutes for press, parliament, and courts. The crisis of India is not only political or economic. The larger crisis is of a wounded old civilization that has at last

become aware of its inadequacies and is without the intellectual means to move ahead.

2

"India will go on." This was what the Indian novelist
R. K. Narayan said to me in London in 1961, before I
had ever been to India.

The novel, which is a form of social inquiry, and as such
outside the Indian tradition, had come to India with the
British. By the late nineteenth century it had become
established in Bengal, and had then spread. But it was only
toward the end of the British period, in the 1930s, that
serious novelists appeared who wrote in English, for first
publication in London. Narayan was one of the earliest and
best of these. He had never been a "political" writer, not
even in the explosive 1930s; and he was unlike many of the
writers after Independence who seemed to regard the novel,
and all writing, as an opportunity for autobiography and
boasting.

Narayan's concern had always been with the life of a
small South Indian town, which he peopled book by book.
His conviction in 1961, after fourteen years of independence, that India would go on, whatever the political uncertainties after Mr. Nehru, was like the conviction of his
earliest novels, written in the days of the British, that India
was going on. In the early novels the British conquest is
like a fact of life. The British themselves are far away,
their presence hinted at only in their institutions: the bank,
the mission school. The writer contemplates the lesser life
that goes on below: small men, small schemes, big talk,
limited means: a life so circumscribed that it appears whole

and unviolated, its smallness never a subject for wonder, though India itself is felt to be vast.

In his autobiography, *My Days*, published in 1974, Narayan fills in the background to his novels. This book, though more exotic in content than the novels, is of a piece with them. It is not more politically explicit or exploratory. The southern city of Madras—one of the earliest English foundations in India, the site leased by the East India Company in 1640 from the last remnant of the Vijayanagar kingdom—was where Narayan spent much of his childhood. Madras was part of a region that had long been pacified, was more Hindu than the north, less Islamized, and had had seventy-five years more of peace. It had known no wars, Narayan says, since the days of Clive. When, during the First World War, the roving German battleship *Emden* appeared in the harbor one night, turned on its searchlights, and began shelling the city, people "wondered at the phenomenon of thunder and lightning with a sky full of stars." Some people fled inland. This flight, Narayan says, "was in keeping with an earlier move, when the sea was rough with cyclone and it was prophesied that the world would end that day."

The world of Narayan's childhood was one that had turned in on itself, had become a world of prophecy and magic, removed from great events and removed, it might seem, from the possibility of politics. But politics did come; and it came, as perhaps it could only come, by stealth, and mingled with ritual and religion. At school Narayan joined the Boy Scouts. But the Boy Scout movement in Madras was controlled by Annie Besant, the Theosophist, who had a larger idea of Indian civilization than most Indians had at that time; and, in sly subversion of Lord Baden-Powell's

imperial purpose, the Besant Scouts sang, to the tune of
"God Save the King": "God save our motherland, God
save our noble land, God save our Ind."

One day in 1919 Narayan fell in with a procession that
had started from the ancient temple of Iswara. The procession sang "patriotic songs" and shouted slogans and
made its way back to the temple, where there was a distribution of sweets. This festive and devout affair was the first
nationalist agitation in Madras. And—though Narayan
doesn't say it—it was part of the first all-India protest that
had been decreed by Gandhi, aged forty-nine, just three
years back from South Africa, and until then relatively
unknown in India. Narayan was pleased to have taken part
in the procession. But his uncle, a young man and a modern
man (one of the earliest amateur photographers in India),
was less than pleased. The uncle, Narayan says, was "anti-
political and did not want me to be misled. He condemned
all rulers, governments and administrative machinery as Sa-
tanic and saw no logic in seeking a change of rulers."

Well, that was where we all began, all of us who are
over forty and were colonials, subject people who had
learned to live with the idea of subjection. We lived within
our lesser world; and we could even pretend it was whole
because we had forgotten that it had been shattered. Disturbance, instability, development lay elsewhere; we, who
had lost our wars and were removed from great events,
were at peace. In life, as in literature, we received tourists.
Subjection flattened, made dissimilar places alike. Narayan's
India, with its colonial apparatus, was oddly like the Trinidad of my childhood. His oblique perception of that
apparatus, and the rulers, matched my own; and in the
Indian life of his novels I found echoes of the life of my
own Indian community on the other side of the world.

But Narayan's novels did not prepare me for the distress of India. As a writer he had succeeded almost too well. His comedies were of the sort that requires a restricted social setting with well-defined rules; and he was so direct, his touch so light, that, though he wrote in English of Indian manners, he had succeeded in making those exotic manners quite ordinary. The small town he had staked out as his fictional territory was, I knew, a creation of art and therefore to some extent artificial, a simplification of reality. But the reality was cruel and overwhelming. In the books his India had seemed accessible; in India it remained hidden. To get down to Narayan's world, to perceive the order and continuity he saw in the dereliction and smallness of India, to enter into his ironic acceptance and relish his comedy, was to ignore too much of what could be seen, to shed too much of myself: my sense of history, and even the simplest ideas of human possibility. I did not lose my admiration for Narayan; but I felt that his comedy and irony were not quite what they had appeared to be, were part of a Hindu response to the world, a response I could no longer share. And it has since become clear to me— especially on this last visit, during a slow rereading of Narayan's 1949 novel, *Mr. Sampath*—that, for all their delight in human oddity, Narayan's novels are less the purely social comedies I had once taken them to be than religious books, at times religious fables, and intensely Hindu.

Srinivas, the hero of *Mr. Sampath*, is a contemplative idler. He has tried many jobs—agriculture, a bank, teaching, the law: the jobs of pre-Independence India: the year is 1938—and rejected all. He stays in his room in the family house—the house of the Indian extended family—and worries about the passing of time. Srinivas's elder brother, a lawyer, looks after the house, and that means he looks after Srinivas and Srinivas's wife and son. The fact that Srinivas has a family is as much a surprise as Srinivas's age: he is thirty-seven.

One day Srinivas is reading the *Upanishads* in his room. His elder brother comes in and says, "What exactly is it that you wish to do in life?" Srinivas replies; "Don't you see? There are ten principal *Upanishads*. I should like to complete the series. This is the third." But Srinivas takes the hint. He decides to go to the town of Malgudi and set up a weekly paper. In Malgudi he lives in a squalid rented room in a crowded lane, bathes at a communal water tap, and finds an office for his paper in a garret.

Srinivas is now in the world, with new responsibilities and new relationships—his landlord, his printer, his wife ("he himself wondered that he had observed so little of her in their years of married life")—but he sees more and more clearly the perfection of nondoing. "While he thundered against municipal or social shortcomings a voice went on asking: 'Life and the world and all this is passing—why bother about anything? The perfect and the imperfect are all the same. Why really bother?' "

His speculations seem idle, and are presented as half comic; but they push him deeper into quietism. From his little room one day he hears the cry of a woman selling vegetables in the lane. Wondering first about her and her customers, and then about the "great human forces" that meet or clash every day, Srinivas has an intimation of the "multitudinousness and vastness of the whole picture of life," and is dazzled. God, he thinks, is to be perceived in that "total picture"; and later, in that total picture, he also perceives a wonderful balance. "If only one could get a comprehensive view of all humanity, one would get a correct view of the world: things being neither particularly wrong nor right, but just balancing themselves." There is really no need to interfere, to do anything. And from this Srinivas moves easily, after a tiff with his wife one day, to a fuller comprehension of Gandhian nonviolence. "Nonviolence in all matters, little or big, personal or national, it seemed to produce an unagitated, undisturbed calm, both in a personality and in society."

But this nonviolence or nondoing depends on society going on; it depends on the doing of others. When Srinivas's printer closes his shop, Srinivas has to close his paper. Srinivas then, through the printer (who is the Mr. Sampath of Narayan's title), finds himself involved as a scriptwriter in the making of an Indian religious film. Srinivas is now deeper than ever in the world, and he finds it chaotic and corrupt. Pure ideas are mangled; sex and farce, song and dance and South American music are grafted onto a story of Hindu gods. The printer, now a kind of producer, falls in love with the leading lady. An artist is in love with her as well. The printer wins, the artist literally goes mad. All is confusion; the film is never made.

Srinivas finally withdraws. He finds another printer and starts his paper again, and the paper is no longer the comic thing it had first seemed. Srinivas has, in essence, returned to himself and to his contemplative life. From this security (and with the help of some rupees sent him by his brother: always the rupees: the rupees are always necessary) Srinivas sees "adulthood" as a state of nonsense, without innocence or pure joy, the nonsense given importance only by "the values of commerce."

There remains the artist, made mad by love and his contact with the world of nonsense. He has to be cured, and there is a local magician who knows what has to be done. He is summoned, and the antique rites begin, which will end with the ceremonial beating of the artist. Tribal, Srinivas thinks: they might all be in the twentieth century B.C. But the oppression he feels doesn't last. Thinking of the primitive past, he all at once has a vision of the millennia of Indian history, and of all the things that might have happened on the ground where they stand.

There, in what would then have been forest, he sees enacted an episode from the Hindu epic of the *Ramayana*, which partly reflects the Aryan settlement of India (perhaps 1000 B.C.). Later, the Buddha (about 560–480 B.C.) comforts a woman whose child has died: "Bring me a handful of mustard seed from a house where no one has died." The philosopher Shankaracharya (A.D. 788–820), preaching the Vedanta on his all-India mission, founds a temple after seeing a spawning frog being sheltered from the sun by its natural enemy, the cobra. And then the missionaries from Europe come, and the merchants, and the soldiers, and Mr. Shilling, who is the manager of the British bank which is now just down the road.

"Dynasties rose and fell. Palaces and mansions appeared and disappeared. The entire country went down under the fire and sword of the invader, and was washed clean when Sarayu overflowed its bounds. But it always had its rebirth and growth." Against this, what is the madness of one man? "Half the madness was his own doing, his lack of self-knowledge, his treachery to his own instincts as an artist, which had made him a battleground. Sooner or later he shook off his madness and realized his true identity— though not in one birth, at least in a series of them . . . Madness or sanity, suffering or happiness seemed all the same . . . in the rush of eternity nothing mattered."

So the artist is beaten, and Srinivas doesn't interfere; and when afterward the magician orders the artist to be taken to a distant temple and left outside the gateway for a week, Srinivas decides that it doesn't matter whether the artist is looked after or not during that time, whether he lives or dies. "Even madness passes," Srinivas says in his spiritual elation. "Only existence asserts itself."

Out of a superficial reading of the past, then, out of the sentimental conviction that India is eternal and forever revives, there comes not a fear of further defeat and destruction, but an indifference to it. India will somehow look after itself; the individual is freed of all responsibility. And within this larger indifference there is the indifference to the fate of a friend: it is madness, Srinivas concludes, for him to think of himself as the artist's keeper.

Just twenty years have passed between Gandhi's first call for civil disobedience and the events of the novel. But already, in Srinivas, Gandhian nonviolence has degenerated into something very like the opposite of what Gandhi intended. For Srinivas nonviolence isn't a form of action, a quickener of social conscience. It is only a means of securing an undisturbed calm; it is nondoing, noninterference, social indifference. It merges with the ideal of self-realization, truth to one's identity. These modern-sounding words, which reconcile Srinivas to the artist's predicament, disguise an acceptance of *karma,* the Hindu killer, the Hindu calm, which tells us that we pay in this life for what we have done in past lives: so that everything we see is just and balanced, and the distress we see is to be relished as religious theater, a reminder of our duty to ourselves, our future lives.

Srinivas's quietism—compounded of *karma,* nonviolence, and a vision of history as an extended religious fable—

is in fact a form of self-cherishing in the midst of a general distress. It is parasitic. It depends on the continuing activity of others, the trains running, the presses printing, the rupees arriving from somewhere. It needs the world, but it surrenders the organization of the world to others. It is a religious response to worldly defeat.

Because we take to novels our own ideas of what we feel they must offer, we often find, in unusual or original work, only what we expect to find, and we reject or miss what we aren't looking for. But it astonished me that, twenty years before, not having been to India, taking to *Mr. Sampath* only my knowledge of the Indian community of Trinidad and my reading of other literature, I should have missed or misread so much, should have seen only a comedy of small-town life and a picaresque, wandering narrative in a book that was really so mysterious.

Now, reading *Mr. Sampath* again in snatches on afternoons of rain during this prolonged monsoon, which went on and on like the Emergency itself—reading in Bombay, looking down at the choppy sea, and the 1911 Imperial rhetoric of the British-built Gateway of India that dwarfed the white-clad crowd; in suburban and secretive New Delhi, looking out across the hotel's sodden tennis court to the encampment of Sikh taxi-drivers below the dripping trees; on the top veranda of the Circuit House in Kotah, considering the garden, and seeing in mango tree and banana tree the originals of the stylized vegetation in the miniatures done for Rajput princes, their glory now extinguished, their great forts now abandoned and empty, protecting nothing, their land now only a land of peasants; in Bangalore in the south, a former British army town, looking across the parade ground, now the polo ground, with Indian army polo teams

—reading during the Emergency, which was more than political, I saw in *Mr. Sampath* a foreshadowing of the tensions that had to come to India, philosophically prepared for defeat and withdrawal (each man an island) rather than independence and action, and torn now between the wish to preserve and be psychologically secure, and the need to undo.

From the *Indian Express*:

New Delhi, Sept 2 . . . Inaugurating the 13th conference of the chairmen and members of the State Social Welfare Advisory Boards here, Mrs. Gandhi said stress on the individual was India's strength as well as weakness. It had given the people an inner strength but had also put a veil between the individual and others in society. . . . Mrs. Gandhi said no social welfare programme could succeed unless the basic attitudes of mind change. . . . "We must live in this age," Mrs. Gandhi said, adding that this did not mean that "we must sweep away" all our past. While people must know of the past, they must move towards the future, she added.

The two ideas—responsibility, the past—were apparently unrelated. But in India they hung together. The speech might have served as a commentary on *Mr. Sampath*. What had seemed speculative and comic, aimless and "Russian" about Narayan's novel had turned out to be something else, the expression of an almost hermetic philosophical system. The novel I had read as a novel was also a fable, a classic exposition of the Hindu equilibrium, surviving the shock of an alien culture, an alien literary form, an alien language, and making harmless even those new concepts it appeared to welcome. Identity became an aspect of *karma*, self-love was bolstered by an ideal of nonviolence.

3

To arrive at an intellectual comprehension of this equilibrium—as some scholars do, working in the main from
Hindu texts—is one thing. To enter into it, when faced
with the Indian reality, is another. The hippies of Western
Europe and the United States appear to have done so; but
they haven't. Out of security and mental lassitude, an intellectual anorexia, they simply cultivate squalor. And their
calm can easily turn to panic. When the price of oil rises
and economies tremble at home, they clean up and bolt.
Theirs is a shallow narcissism; they break just at that point
where the Hindu begins: the knowledge of the abyss, the
acceptance of distress as the condition of men.

It is out of an eroded human concern, rather than the
sentimental wallow of the hippies and others who "love"
India, that a dim understanding begins to come. And it
comes at those moments when, in spite of all that has been
done since Independence, it seems that enough will never
be done; and despair turns to weariness, and thoughts of
action fade. Such a moment came to me this time in North
Bihar. Bihar, for centuries the cultural heartland of India
("Bihar" from vihara, a Buddhist monastery), now without
intellect or leaders: in the south a land of drought and
famine and flood, in the north a green, well-watered land of
jute (like tall reeds) and paddy and fishponds.

In the village I went to, only one family out of four had
land; only one child out of four went to school; only one
man out of four had work. For a wage calculated to keep
him only in food for the day he worked, the employed man,
hardly exercising a skill, using the simplest tools and sometimes no tools at all, did the simplest agricultural labor.

Child's work; and children, being cheaper than men, were preferred; so that, suicidally, in the midst of an over-population which no one recognized (an earthquake in 1935 had shaken down the population, according to the villagers, and there had been a further thinning out during the floods of 1971), children were a source of wealth, available for hire after their eighth year for, if times were good, fifteen rupees, a dollar fifty, a month.

Generation followed generation quickly here, men as easily replaceable as their huts of grass and mud and matting (golden when new, quickly weathering to gray-black). Cruelty no longer had a meaning; it was life itself. Men knew what they were born to. Every man knew his caste, his place; each group lived in its own immemorially defined area; and the pariahs, the scavengers, lived at the end of the village. Above the huts rose the rambling two-story brick mansion of the family who had once owned it all, the land and the people: grandeur that wasn't grandeur, but was like part of the squalor and defeat out of which it had arisen. The family was now partially dispossessed, but, as politicians, they still controlled. Nothing had changed or seemed likely to change.

And during the rest of that day's drive North Bihar repeated itself: the gray-black hut clusters; the green paddy fields whose luxuriance and springlike freshness can deceive earth-scanners and cause yields to be overestimated; the bare-backed men carrying loads on either end of a long limber pole balanced on their shoulders, the strain showing in their brisk, mincing walk, which gave them a curious feminine daintiness; the overcrowded buses at dusty towns that were shack settlements; the children wallowing in the muddy ponds in the heat of the day, catching fish; the children and the men pounding soaked jute stalks to extract the fiber which, loaded on bullock carts, looked like thick plaited blond tresses, immensely rich. Thoughts of human possibility dwindled; North Bihar seemed to have become the world, capable only of the life that was seen.

It was like the weariness I had felt some weeks before, in the Bundi-Kotah region of Rajasthan, eight hundred miles to the west. If in North Bihar there had seemed to be, with the absence of intellect and creativity, an absence almost of administration, here in Rajasthan was prodigious enterprise. Here were dams and a great irrigation-and-reclamation scheme in a land cut up and wasted by ravines.

Imperfectly conceived twenty years before—no drainage, the nature of the soil not taken into account—the irrigation scheme had led to waterlogging and salinity. Now, urgently, this was being put right. There was a special commissioner, and he and his deputies were men of the utmost energy. The technical problems could be solved. The difficulties—in this state of desert forts, feudal princes, and a peasantry trained only in loyalty, equipped for little else—lay with the people: not just with the "mediocrity at every level" which the commissioner said he found in the administration, but also with the people lower down, whom the scheme was meant to benefit. How could they, used for generations to so little, content to find glory only in the glory of their rulers, be made now, almost suddenly, to want, to do?

The commissioner's powers were great, but he was unwilling to rule despotically; he wished to "institutionalize." One evening, by the light of an electric bulb—electricity in the village!—we sat out with the villagers in the main street of a "model village" of the command area. The street was unpaved, and the villagers, welcoming us, had quickly spread cotton rugs on the ground that had been softened by the morning's rain, half hardened by the afternoon's heat, and then trampled and manured by the village cattle returning at dusk. The women had withdrawn—so many of them, below their red or orange Rajasthani veils, only girls, children, but already with children of their own. We were left with the men; and, until the rain came roaring in again, we talked.

So handsome, these men of Rajasthan, so self-possessed: it took time to understand that they were only peasants, and limited. The fields, water, crops, cattle: that was where concern began and ended. They were a model village, and so they considered themselves. There was little more that they needed, and I began to see my own ideas of village improvement as fantasies. Nothing beyond food—and survival —had as yet become an object of ambition; though one man said, fantastically, that he would like a telephone, to find out about the price of grain in Kotah without having to go there.

The problems of the irrigation project were not only those of salinity or the ravines or land-leveling. The problem, as the commissioner saw, was the remaking of men. And this was not simply making men want; it meant, in the first place, bringing them back from the self-wounding and the special waste that come with an established destitution. We were among men who, until recently, cut only the very tops of sugar cane and left the rest of the plant, the substance of the crop, to rot. So this concern about fertilizers and yields, this acquiring by the villagers of what I had at first judged to be only peasant attributes, was an immeasurable advance.

But if in this model village—near Kotah Town, which

was fast industrializing—there had been some movement, Bundi the next day seemed to take us backward. Bundi and Kotah: to me, until this trip, they had only been beautiful names, the names of related but distinct schools of Rajasthan painting. The artistic glory of Bundi had come first, in the late seventeenth century. And after the flat waterlogged fields, pallid paddy thinning out at times to marshland, after the desolation of the road from Kotah, the flooded ditches, the occasional cycle-rickshaw, the damp groups of bright-turbaned peasants waiting for the bus, Bundi Castle on its hill was startling, its great walls like the work of giants, the extravagant creation of men who had once had much to defend.

Old wars, bravely fought; but usually little more had been at stake than the honor and local glory of one particular prince. The fortifications were now useless, the palace was empty. One dark, dusty room had old photographs and remnants of Victorian bric-a-bric. The small formal garden in the courtyard was in decay; and the mechanical, decorative nineteenth-century Bundi murals around the courtyard had faded to blues and yellows and greens. In the inner rooms, hidden from the sun, brighter colors survived, and some panels were exquisite. But it all awaited ruin. The monsoon damp was rotting away plaster; water dripped through green-black cracks in underground arches; and the sharp smell of bat dung was everywhere.

All vitality had been sucked up into that palace on the hill; and now vitality had gone out of Bundi. It showed in the rundown town on the hillside below the palace; it showed in the fields; it showed in the people, more beaten down than at Kotah Town just sixty miles away, less amenable to the commissioner's ideas, and more full of complaints. They complained even when they had no cause; and it seemed that they complained because they felt it was expected of them. Their mock aggressiveness and mock desperation held little of real despair or rebellion. It was a ritual show of deference to authority, a demonstration of their complete dependence on authority. The commissioner smiled and listened and heard them all; and their passion faded.

Later we sat with the "village-level workers" in the shade of a small tree in a woman's yard. These officials were the last in the chain of command; on them much of the success of the scheme depended. There had been evidence during the morning's tour that they hadn't all been doing their jobs. But they were not abashed; instead, sitting in a line on a string bed, dressed not like the peasants that they almost were, but dressed like officials, in trousers and shirts, they spoke of their need for promotion and status. They were far removed from the commissioner's anxieties, from his vision of what could be done with their land. They were, really, at peace with the world they knew. Like the woman in whose yard we sat. She was friendly, she had dragged out string beds for us from her little brick hut; but her manner was slightly supercilious. There was a reason. She was happy, she considered herself blessed. She had had three sons, and she glowed with that achievement.

All the chivalry of Rajasthan had been reduced here to nothing. The palace was empty; the petty wars of princes had been absorbed into legend and could no longer be dated. All that remained was what the visitor could see: small, poor fields, ragged men, huts, monsoon mud. But in that very abjectness lay security. Where the world had shrunk, and ideas of human possibility had become extinct, the world could be seen as complete. Men had retreated to their last, impregnable defenses: their knowledge of who they were, their caste, their *karma*, their unshakable place in the scheme of things; and this knowledge was like their knowledge of the seasons. Rituals marked the passage of each day; rituals marked every stage of a man's life. Life itself had been turned to ritual; and everything beyond this complete and sanctified world—where fulfillment came so easily to a man or to a woman—was vain and phantasmal.

Kingdoms, empires, projects like the commissioner's: they had come and gone. The monuments of ambition and restlessness littered the land, so many of them abandoned or destroyed, so many unfinished, the work of dynasties suddenly supplanted. India taught the vanity of all action; and the visitor could be appalled by the waste, and by all that now appeared to threaten the commissioner's enterprise.

But to those who embraced its philosophy of distress India also offered an enduring security, its equilibrium, that vision of a world finely balanced that had come to the hero of *Mr. Sampath*, that "arrangement made by the gods." Only India, with its great past, its civilization, its philosophy, and its almost holy poverty, offered this truth; India *was* the truth. So, to Indians, India could detach itself from the rest of the world. The world could be divided into India and non-India. And India, for all its surface terrors, could be proclaimed, without disingenuousness or cruelty, as perfect. Not only by pauper, but by prince.

4

Consider this prince, in another part of the country, far from the castles of Rajasthan. Another landscape, another type of vegetation; only, the rain continued. The princes of India—their number and variety reflecting to a large extent the chaos that had come to the country with the break-up of the Mughal empire—had lost real power in the British time. Through generations of idle servitude they had grown to specialize only in style. A bogus, extinguishable glamour: in 1947, with Independence, they had lost their states, and Mrs. Gandhi in 1971 had, without much public outcry, abolished their privy purses and titles. The power of this prince had continued; he had become an energetic entrepreneur. But in his own eyes, and in the eyes of those who served him, he remained a prince. And perhaps his grief for his title, and his insistence on his dignity, was the greater because his state had really been quite small, a fief of some hundred square miles, granted three centuries before to an ancestor, a soldier of fortune.

With his buttoned-up Indian tunic, the prince was quite the autocrat at the dinner table, down the middle of which ran an arrangement of chiffon stuck with roses; and it was some time before I saw that he had come down drunk to our teetotal dinner. He said, unprompted, that he was "observing" the crisis of Indian democracy with "interest." India needed Indian forms of government; India wasn't one country, but hundreds of little countries. I thought he was building up the case for his own autocratic rule. But his conversational course—almost a soliloquy—was wilder.

"What keeps a country together? Not economics. Love. Love and affection. That's our Indian way. . . . You can feed my dog, but he won't obey you. He'll obey me. Where's the economics in that? That's love and affection. . . . For twenty-eight years until 1947 I ruled this state. Power of life and death. Could have hanged a man and nobody could have done anything to me. . . . Now they've looted my honor, my privilege. I'm nobody. I'm just like everybody else. . . . Power of life and death. But I can still go out and walk. Nobody's going to try and kill me like Kennedy. That's not economics. That's our love and affection. . . . Where's the cruelty you talk about? I tell you, we're *happy* in India. . . . Who's talking about patriotism? Have no cause to be. Took away everything. Honor, titles, all looted. I'm not a patriot, but I'm an Indian. Go out and talk to the people. They're poor, but they're not inhuman, as you say. . . . You people must leave us alone. You mustn't come and tell us we're subhuman. We're civilized. Are they happy where you come from? Are they happy in England?"

In spite of myself, my irritation was rising. I said: "They're very happy in England." He broke off and laughed. But he had spoken seriously. He was acting a little, but he believed everything he said.

His state, or what had been his state, was wretched: just the palace (like a country house, with a garden) and the peasants. The development (in which he had invested) hadn't yet begun to show. In the morning in the rain I saw young child laborers using their hands alone to shovel gravel onto a waterlogged path. Groundnuts were the only source of protein here; but the peasants preferred to sell their crop; and their children were stunted, their minds deformed, serf material already, beyond the reach of education where that was available.

(But science, a short time later, was to tell me otherwise. From the *Indian Express*: "New Delhi, Nov. 2 . . . Delivering the Dr. V. N. Patwardhan Prize oration at the India Council of Medical Research yesterday, Dr. Kamala Rao said certain hormonal changes within the body of the malnourished children enabled them to maintain normal body functions. . . . Only the excess and nonessential parts of the body are affected by malnutrition. Such malnourished children, though small in size, are like 'paperback books' which, while retaining all the material of the original, have got rid of the nonessential portion of the bound editions.")

The prince had traveled outside India. He was in a position to compare what he had seen outside with what he could see of his own state. But the question of comparison did not arise. The world outside India was to be judged by its own standards. India was not to be judged. India was only to be experienced, in the Indian way. And when the prince spoke of the happiness of his people, he was not being provocative or backward-looking. As an entrepreneur, almost an industrialist, he saw himself as a benefactor. When he talked about love and affection, he did not exaggerate: he needed to be loved as much as he needed to be reverenced. His attachment to his people was real. And his attachment to the land went beyond that.

In the unpopulated, forested hills some miles away from the palace there was an old temple. The temple was small and undistinguished. Its sculptures had weathered to unrecognizable knobs and indentations; the temple tank or reservoir was overgrown and reedy, the wide stone steps had sagged into the milky-green slime. But the temple was important to the prince. His ancestors had adopted the deity of the temple as their own, and the family maintained the priest. It was an ancient site; it had its genius; the whole place was still in worship. India offered the prince not only the proofs of his princehood but also this abiding truth of his relationship to the earth, the universe.

In this ability to separate India from what was not India, the prince was like the middle-class (and possibly rich) girl I met at a Delhi dinner party. She was married to a foreigner and lived abroad. This living abroad was glamorous; when she spoke of it, she appeared to be boasting, in the Indian fashion: she detached herself from the rest of India. But for the Indian woman a foreign marriage is seldom a positive act; it is, more usually, an act of despair or confusion. It leads to castelessness, the loss of community, the loss of a place in the world; and few Indians are equipped to cope with that.

Socially and intellectually this girl, outside India, was an innocent. She had no means of assessing her alien society; she lived in a void. She needed India and all its reassurances, and she came back to India whenever she could. India didn't jar, she said; and then, remembering to boast, she added, "I relate only to my family."

Such security! In the midst of world change, India, even during this Emergency, was unchanging: to return to India was to return to a knowledge of the world's deeper order, everything fixed, sanctified, everyone secure. Like a sleepwalker, she moved without disturbance between her two opposed worlds. But surely the streets of Bombay must make some impression? What did she see at the moment of arrival?

She said mystically, blankly, and with truth, "I see people having their being."

2

The Shattering World

1

"India will go on," the novelist R. K. Narayan had said
in 1961. And for the prince with his ancestral pieties, the
girl with her foreign marriage, the peasant of Bihar or
Bundi with his knowledge of *karma*, India was going on:
the Hindu equilibrium still held. They were as removed
from the Emergency in 1975 as Narayan himself had been
from the political uncertainties of 1961.

Narayan was then in his fifties. Living in India, writing
in English for publication abroad, operating as a novelist
in a culture where the idea of the novel was new and as yet
little understood, Narayan had had to wait long for recognition. He was middle-aged, the best of his work done, his
fictional world established, before he had traveled out of
India; and when I met him in London, this late travel
seemed to have brought him no shocks.

He had just been visiting the United States, and was
returning happily to India. He said he needed to go again
for his afternoon walks, to be among his characters, the

people he wrote about. In literature itself he was not so interested. Like his hero in *Mr. Sampath*, he was letting his thoughts turn to the Infinite; in the midst of activity and success, he was preparing, in the Hindu way, for withdrawal. He said he had begun to read sacred Sanskrit texts with the help of a pundit. He seemed a man at peace with his world, at peace with India and the fictional world he had abstracted from the country.

But it was in the 1930s, before Independence, that Narayan had established his fictional world: the small and pacific South Indian town, little men, little schemes, the comedy of restricted lives and high philosophical speculation, real power surrendered long ago to the British rulers, who were far away and only dimly perceived. With Independence, however, the world had grown larger around Narayan. Power had come closer; men were required to be bigger. To Narayan himself had come recognition and foreign travel; and though in the red land around Bangalore, one of the cities of Narayan's childhood, peasant life continued as it had always done, Bangalore was becoming a center of Indian industry and science.

Narayan's small town could not easily be insulated from the larger, restless world, could no longer be seen as finished and complete, with the well-defined boundaries necessary for his kind of humor. And very soon, after the certitude of 1961, doubt seemed to have come to Narayan. As early as 1967 there appeared a novel in which his fictional world is cracked open, its fragility finally revealed, and the Hindu equilibrium—so confidently maintained in *Mr. Sampath*—collapses into something like despair.

The novel is *The Vendor of Sweets*. It is not one of Narayan's better books; but Narayan is such a natural writer, so true to his experience and emotions, that this novel is as much a key to the moral bewilderment of today as *Mr. Sampath* was to the sterility of Hindu attitudes at the time of Independence. *The Vendor of Sweets*, like *Mr. Sampath*, is a fable, and it broadly repeats the theme of the earlier book: there is a venture into the world of doing, and at the end there is a withdrawal.

The sweet-vendor is Jagan, a rich man, conscientiously adding every day to his money hoard at home (the "black money" of India), but a Gandhian, a faddist, a man obsessed with the idea of purity. He is fair with his customers; he cheats only the government of the country for whose sake, in the British days, he endured police beatings and imprisonment in an insanitary jail. "If Gandhi had said somewhere, 'Pay your sales tax uncomplainingly,' he would have followed his advice, but Gandhi had made no reference to the sales tax anywhere to Jagan's knowledge."

(Was Jagan then a freedom fighter, concerned about the political humiliation of his country, or was he only the disciple of a holy man, in the old Hindu tradition? Hindu morality, centered on the self and self-realization, has its own social corruptions: how many Jagans exist who, conscious only of their Gandhian piety, their personal virtue, have mocked and undermined the Independence for which tney say they have worked! But Narayan doesn t raise the point. He only makes the joke about Gandhi and the sales tax; he is on Jagan's side.)

Jagan is a widower with one child, a son, on whom he dotes. The boy, though, is sullen and talks little to his father. He announces one day that he is finished with school: he wants to be a writer. And later Jagan discovers that the boy, using money from the money hoard at home, has booked his passage to the United States, to go to a school of creative writing. Jagan digests his disappointment; the boy goes away. Very quickly, the time passes; and then, almost without warning, the boy returns. He is not alone. He is with a woman, apparently his wife, who, startlingly in that South Indian setting, is half Korean, half American. Between them they have plans, and they need Jagan's money. They have come to India to set up, with American collaboration, a factory which will manufacture story-writing machines. It is an American invention; and, like Americans, the couple bustle about the ramshackle little town.

The satire is too gross, the newcomers too outlandish. Comedy fails, and the writer's fictional world collapses, for the reasons that Jagan's world collapses: they have both been damaged by the intrusion of alien elements. Shock follows shock. The boy fusses about the absence of a telephone, rides about on a scooter (Jagan is content to walk), speaks contemptuously of the sweet shop. It also turns out that he is not married to the woman, who, not being Indian, is already casteless and therefore without a place in Jagan's world. All the rules have been broken; Jagan is lost. Without a vision of the future now, he can only contemplate the sweet rituals of the recent, ordered past: his childhood, his marriage, a pilgrimage to a temple.

He feels that his home has been "dirtied," and at last he recoils. He barricades himself against the couple; he seeks, with a "peculiar excitement," to purify himself. He begins to sell his sweets cheaply to the poor and offends the other shopkeepers; he assembles his staff and reads the *Gita* aloud to them. Finally he decides to withdraw to a wilderness away from the town, near a ruined shrine. There, divested of possessions, he will watch a master carver, who is like a "man from the previous millennium," complete an old, unfinished image of a five-faced goddess, "the light that illumines the sun itself."

Before he can withdraw, the Korean girl leaves. Jagan's son, getting nowhere with his business plans, has decided to send her away. And then the son himself is arrested for having a bottle of liquor in his car. Under the prohibition laws he faces two years in jail. For Jagan this is the final blow, not so much the threat of the jail sentence as the news that his son drinks. He weeps; he will of course pay for lawyers for his son; but he is more determined than ever to give up the world. "A little prison life won't harm any-one," he says. "Who are we to get him out or put him in?" And he goes to take the bus out of town, on the way to his jungle retreat.

So, with high virtue, Jagan abandons his son, just as Srinivas, the hero of *Mr. Sampath*, "elated" by his vision of eternity, abandoned his friend. But it was only from the world of commerce and "nonsense" that Srinivas withdrew. Jagan's flight is not like Srinivas's withdrawal, and is the opposite of the calm renunciation which Hinduism pre-scribes, when the householder, his duties done, makes way for his successors and turns to a life of meditation. That act of renunciation implies an ordered, continuing world. Chaos has come to Jagan's world; his act is an act of despair; he runs away in tears.

"The entire country went down under the fire and sword of the invader. . . . But it always had its rebirth and growth." This was how, in pre-Independence India, the hero of *Mr. Sampath* saw the course of Indian history: rebirth and growth as a cleansing, a recurrent Indian miracle, brought about only by the exercise of self-knowledge. But in independent India rebirth and growth have other meanings and call for another kind of effort. The modern world, after all, cannot be caricatured or conjured away; a pastoral past cannot be reestablished.

Bangalore, the capital city of the state which contains Narayan's fictional small town, is also India's scientific capital. In 1961—when Narayan told me that India would go on—there were perhaps two scientists of distinction at work in Bangalore. Today, I was told, there are twenty. It was at Bangalore that the first Indian space satellite (named, typically, after a medieval Hindu astronomer) was built: more impressive as a scientific achievement, it is said, than the Indian atomic bomb, more revealing of the technological capacity that India has developed since Independence. The dedicated chief secretary of the state, a man of simple origins, sees himself and his family as the products both of Independence and of India's industrial revolution. He is committed to that revolution; the changes it is bringing about, he says, are "elemental."

From Bangalore there runs a five-hundred-mile highway through the Deccan plateau to Poona, the industrial town on the edge of the plateau east of Bombay. There are almost no cars on this highway, many bullock carts, many lorries. The lorries are hideously overloaded; their tires are worn smooth; and the lorries often overturn. But, through all the old pain of rural India, the industrial traffic is constant. Change has indeed come to people like Jagan; their world cannot be made small again.

But what to the administrator is elemental change, and urgently necessary, can also be seen as violation. Narayan is an instinctive, unstudied writer: the lack of balance in

The Vendor of Sweets, the loss of irony, and the very crudity of the satire on "modern" civilization speak of the depth of the violation Narayan feels that that civilization —in its Indian aspect—has brought to someone like Jagan. And how fragile that Hindu world turns out to be, after all! From the outside so stable and unyielding, yet liable to crumble at the first assault from within: the self-assertion of a son to whom has come a knowledge of the larger world, another, non-Hindu idea of human possibility, and who is no longer content to be part of the flow, part of the Hindu continuity.

Some of the gestures of rebellion might seem trivial— driving in motorcars, meat-eating, drinking—but to Jagan they are all momentous. Where ritual regulates the will and so much of behavior is ceremonial, all gestures are important. One gesture of rebellion, as Narayan seems to suggest, brings others in its train, and very quickly they add up to a rejection of the piety and reverences that held the society together, a rejection of *karma*. Such a fragile world, where rebellion is so easy, a mere abandoning of ritual! It is as though the Hindu equilibrium required a world as small and as restricting as that of Narayan's early novels, where men could never grow, talked much and did little, and were fundamentally obedient, content to be ruled in all things by others. As soon as that world expands, it shatters.

The Vendor of Sweets, which is so elegiac and simplistic, exalting purity and old virtue in the figure of Jagan, is a confused book; and its confusion holds much of the Indian confusion today. Jagan—unlike the hero of *Mr. Sampath* in pre-Independence India—really has no case. His code does not bear examination.

Everything rests on his Gandhianism. Jagan, as we are often reminded, was a Gandhian "volunteer" and freedom fighter in his time; and once, during a demonstration, he allowed himself to be beaten unconscious by the police. It was the genius of Gandhi: intuiting just where the Hindu virtues of quietism and religious self-cherishing could be converted into selfless action of overwhelming political force. Jagan, allowing himself to be beaten, finding in the violence offered him a confirmation of his own virtue, saw himself as a *satyagrahi*, "fighting for the truth against the British." The stress was on the fight for the truth rather than the fight against the British. Jagan's was a holy war; he had a vision of his country cleansed and purified rather than a political vision of his country remade.

Jagan won his war. Now, blinded by this victory to his own worldly corruption (the corruption that, multiplied a million times, has taken his country in Independence to another kind of political collapse), his Gandhian impulses decayed to self-cherishing, faddism, and social indifference, Jagan seeks only to maintain the stability of his world; he is capable of nothing else. To be pure in the midst of "the grime of this earth," secure in the midst of distress: that is all he asks. When his world shatters, he cannot fight back; he has nothing to offer. He can only run away. Another Hindu retreat—like the Vijayanagar kingdom in 1336, like the pilgrims worshiping among the ruins of the Vijayanagar capital in 1975, like the *mantra* being chanted and written fifty million times to give life to the new image of the temple defiled during the last war.

Jagan's is the ultimate Hindu retreat, because it is a retreat from a world that is known to have broken down at last. It is a retreat, literally, to a wilderness where "the edge of reality itself was beginning to blur": not a return to a purer Aryan past, as Jagan might imagine, but a retreat from civilization and creativity, from rebirth and growth, to magic and incantation, a retrogression to an almost African night, the enduring primitivism of a place like the Congo, where, even after the slave-trading Arabs and the Belgians, the past is yearned for as *le bon vieux temps de nos ancêtres*. It is the death of a civilization, the final corruption of Hinduism.

2

With the Emergency, there was a "clean-up." And it was on this, rather than the political crisis, that the censored press concentrated.

The former Maharani of Jaipur was then in jail, charged with economic offenses and apparently without the prospect of a quick trial. The houses of the once ruling family of Gwalior were being searched for undeclared treasure. In Bombay the flats of government officials, bank officials, and businessmen—flats the newspapers described as "posh"—were being raided, their contents assessed. Somewhere else —a touch of Hollywood India—an opium-fed cobra was found guarding (ineffectually) a four-kilogram hoard of gold and gold ornaments. Everywhere rackets were being "busted": foreign-exchange dealings, smuggling, black-marketing, the acquiring of steel by bogus manufacturing units, scarce railway wagons shunted onto sidings and used as storage for hoarded commodities.

Panic was general, but not everyone lost his head. One New Delhi businessman (with a brother already raided), when told by his chauffeur that he was next on the list,

handed over all his valuables for safekeeping to the chauffeur, who then vanished. Day by day the censored press
carried communiqués about searches, arrests, suspensions,
and compulsory retirements. By the third week of August,
fifteen hundred smugglers alone were said to have been
picked up. At this inauspicious time an expensive new
jewelry shop opened in the Oberoi-Sheraton Hotel in
Bombay, to big advertisements in the newspapers. Almost
immediately, and as though they had been waiting for the
place to open first, the authorities sealed the doors.

It was an arbitrary terror, reaching out to high and low:
the divisional engineer forging issue vouchers and selling
off the stores of a steel plant, the sales-tax inspector accepting a five-hundred-rupee bribe, fifty dollars, from a small
businessman, the railway servant carrying rice "illegally"
in a dining car, the postman suspected of opening a foreign
packet. And for the moment, after the unrest and drift of
the preceding years, it brought peace to India.

But it was only terror, and it came confused with a political crisis everyone knew about. It established no new
moral frame for the society; it held out no promise for a
better-regulated future. It reinforced, if anything, the always
desperate Hindu sense of the self, the sense of encircling
external threat, the need to hide and hoard. In the high
Hindu ideal of self-realization—which could take so many
forms, even that of worldly corruption—there was no idea
of a contract between man and man. It was Hinduism's
great flaw, after a thousand years of defeat and withdrawal.
And now the society had broken down. It was of that, really,
that the press spoke, rather than of a clean-up, or of an
Emergency, a passing crisis, which it was in the power of
Mrs. Gandhi or the opposition to resolve.

The Emergency, whatever its immediate political promptings, only made formal a state of breakdown that had existed for some time; it needed more than a political resolution. In 1975 the constitution was suspended; but already, in 1974, India had appeared to stall, with civil-disobedience campaigns, strikes, and student disturbances. The political issues were real, but they obscured the bigger crisis. The corruption of which the opposition spoke and indiscipline of which the rulers spoke were both aspects of a moral chaos, and this could be traced back to the beginning, to Independence.

Hindu society, which Gandhi had appeared to ennoble during the struggle for Independence, had begun to disintegrate with the rebirth and growth that had come with Independence. One journalist said that the trouble—he called it the betrayal—had started the day after Independence, when Mr. Nehru, as prime minister, had moved into the former British commander-in-chief's house in New Delhi. But the trouble lay more with the nature of the movement that had brought Mr. Nehru to power, the movement to which Gandhi, by something like magic, had given a mass base. A multitude of Jagans, nationalist but committed only to a holy war, had brought the country Independence. A multitude of Jagans, new to responsibility but with no idea of the state—businessmen, money-hoarding but always pious; politicians, Gandhi-capped and Gandhi-garbed—had worked to undo that Independence. Now the Jagans had begun to be rejected, and India was discovering that it had ceased to be Gandhian.

It was hardly surprising: Gandhian India had been very swiftly created. In just eleven years, between 1919 (when the first Gandhian agitation in Madras had ended with a distribution of sweets in a temple) and 1930 (when the Salt March ended with squads of disciplined volunteers offering themselves, in group after group, to sickening police blows), Gandhi had given India a new idea of itself, and also given the world a new idea of India. In those eleven years nonviolence had been made to appear an ancient, many-sided Indian truth, an eternal source of Hindu action. Now of Gandhianism there remained only the emblems and the energy; and the energy had turned malignant. India needed a new code, but it had none. There were no longer any rules; and India—so often invaded, conquered, plundered, with a quarter of its population always in the serfdom of untouchability, people without a country, only with masters—was discovering again that it was cruel and horribly violent.

In a speech before the Emergency, Jaya Prakash Narayan, the most respected opposition leader, said: "It is not the existence of disputes and quarrels that so much endangers the integrity of the nation as the manner in which we conduct them. We often behave like animals. Be it a village feud, a students' organization, a labor dispute, a religious procession, a boundary disagreement, or a major political question, we are more likely than not to become aggressive, wild, and violent. We kill and burn and loot and sometimes commit even worse crimes."

The violence of the riot could burn itself out; it could be controlled, as it now was, by the provisions of the Emergency. But there was an older, deeper Indian violence. This violence had remained untouched by foreign rule and had survived Gandhi. It had become part of the Hindu social order, and there was a stage at which it became invisible, disappearing in the general distress. But now, with the Emergency, the emphasis was on reform, and on the "weaker sections" of society; and the stories the censored newspapers played up seemed at times to come from another age. A boy seized by a village moneylender for an unpaid debt of 150 rupees, fifteen dollars, and used as a slave for four years; in September, in Vellore in the south, untouchables forced to leave their village after their huts had been fenced in by caste Hindus and their well polluted; in October, in a village in Gujarat in the west, a campaign of terror against untouchables rebelling against forced labor and the plundering of their crops; the custom, among the untouchable men of a northern district, of selling their wives to Delhi brothels to pay off small debts to their caste landlords.

To the ancient Aryans the untouchables were "walking carrion." Gandhi—like other reformers before him—sought to make them part of the holy Hindu system. He called them *Harijans*, children of God. A remarkable linguistic coincidence: they have remained God's chillun. Even at the Satyagraha Ashram on the riverbank at Ahmedabad, which Gandhi himself founded after his return from South Africa, and from where in 1930 he started on the great Salt March. *Son et Lumière* at night these days in the ashram, sponsored by the Tourism Development Corporation; and in the mornings, in one of the buildings, a school for Harijan girls. "Backward class, backward class," the old brahmin, suddenly my guide, explained piously, converting the girls into distant objects of awe. The antique violence remained: rural untouchability as serfdom, maintained by terror and sometimes by deliberate starvation. None of this was new; but suddenly in India it was news.

Mr. Nehru had once observed that a danger in India

was that poverty might be deified. Gandhianism had had that effect. The Mahatma's simplicity had appeared to make poverty holy, the basis of all truth, and a unique Indian possession. And so, for twenty years after Independence, it had more or less remained. It was Mrs. Gandhi, in 1971, who had made poverty a political issue. Her slogan in the election that year had been *Garibi Hatao*, Remove Poverty. Her opponents then, fighting another kind of war, had only replied *Indira Hatao*, Remove Indira. But India had since moved fast. There was now competition in protest. And as a cause for protest the holy poverty of India was all at once seen to be inexhaustible. There seemed always another, lower level of distress.

The government now, committed by the Emergency to radical reform, decreed the quashing of certain kinds of rural debts. Two or three hundred of the moneylenders who had been terrorizing the colliers of the Dhanbad coalfields in Bihar were arrested. And, twenty-eight years after Independence, bonded labor was declared illegal. Bonded labor! In thirteen years I had made three visits to India and had in all spent sixteen months there. I had visited villages in many parts of the country, but I had never heard of bonded labor. An editorial in the *Deccan Herald* of Bangalore suggested why: "The system is as old as life itself. . . . In the country itself, the practice of slavery had attained [such] a sophistication that the victims themselves were made to feel a moral obligation to remain in slavery." *Karma!*

With Independence and growth, chaos and a loss of faith, India was awakening to its distress and the cruelties that had always lain below its apparent stability, its capacity simply for going on. Not everyone now was content simply to have his being. The old equilibrium had gone, and at the moment all was chaos. But out of this chaos, out of the crumbling of the old Hindu system, and the spirit of rejection, India was learning new ways of seeing and feeling.

3

An exponent of the "new morality" of post-Gandhian India is the playwright Vijay Tendulkar. He writes in Marathi, the language of the region around Bombay, but he is translated into other languages. When I was there, an "Indian English" version of his play *The Vultures* was being put on in Bombay. The title says it all: for Tendulkar industrial or industrializing India, bringing economic opportunity to small men (in the play, a family of petty contractors), releasing instincts that poverty had suppressed, undoing old pieties, has become a land of vultures.

It is the theme of *The Vendor of Sweets* again: the end of reverences, the end of the family, individuals striking out on their own, social chaos. But Tendulkar is more violent than Narayan; his India is a crueler, more recognizable place. And though Tendulkar is Hindu enough to suggest, like Narayan, that the loss of one kind of restraint quickly leads to the unraveling of the whole system, and purity is possible only to the man who holds himself aloof, for Tendulkar there is no pure past, and religion can provide no retreat. Tendulkar, for all his brutality, is a romantic: in *The Vultures* the man who holds himself aloof is a poet, an illegitimate son, an outsider.

Tendulkar's India is clearly the same country as Narayan's. But it is a country to which change has come. The world has opened out, and men have become more various and individualistic; the will rages. Sensibility has been modified. India is less mysterious: Tendulkar's discoveries are like those that might be made elsewhere.

The hero of *Sakharam Binder*—Tendulkar's most popular play, which got him into trouble with the censors in 1972, long before the Emergency, and later ran simultaneously in four languages in four Bombay theaters—is a workingman of low caste who has rejected all faith, all ties of community and family. Sakharam stands alone. His material security is the technical skill which gives him his second name: he is a binder in a printing shop. He will not marry (it isn't said, but he will be able to marry only within his caste, and so continue to be categorized and branded); instead, he lives with other men's discarded wives, whom he rescues from temples or the streets (a glimpse, there, of the Indian abyss). Sakharam is not tender or especially gifted; all he insists on being is a man, when he has closed the door on the outside world and is in his own two rooms. Hinduism, in him, has been reduced to a belief in honesty and a rejection of all shaming action. In the end he is destroyed; but he has been presented as heroic.

With Sakharam we have come far from the simple rebellion of Jagan's son in *The Vendor of Sweets*, which could be satirized as un-Indian and a mimicry of Western manners. Sakharam's rebellion goes deeper, is immediately comprehensible, and it is entirely of India. India, coming late to situations that have been lived through elsewhere, becomes less mysterious.

Some time ago Tendulkar was awarded a Nehru Fellowship, and this has enabled him to travel about India, getting material for a book on violence in India. It was news of this project—at first so startling, and then so obvious and

right—that made me want to see him. I put him in his late
forties, one generation younger than Narayan. He was
paunchy and surprisingly placid. But the placidity was
deceptive: his mother had died a few days before our
meeting, and the censors had just blocked a film for which
he had written the script. He said his travels about India
followed no set plan; he simply, now and then, followed
his nose. He had been investigating the Naxalite peasant
movement, which had sought to bring about land reforms
by force, had degenerated in some places into rural terror-
ism, and had been very quickly crushed by the government.
He had been to the Telengana district in the south, and to
Bihar and West Bengal in the northeast.

Bihar had depressed Tendulkar especially. He had seen
things there that he had never believed existed. But he
didn't speak more precisely: it was as though he still felt
humiliated by what he had seen. He said only, "The
human relationships. They're so horrible because they are
accepted by the victims." New words, new concerns: and
still, even for a writer like Tendulkar, the discovery of India
could be like the discovery of a foreign country. He said
he had traveled about Bihar by boat, down the Ganges.
And it was of the serenity that came to him on this river,
sacred to Hindus, that he spoke, rather than of the horrors
on the bank.

So it was still there, and perhaps always would be, in
the pain of India: the yearning for calm, the area of retreat.
But men cannot easily unlearn new modes of feeling.
Retreat is no longer possible. Even the ashrams and the
holy men (with their executive jets, their international
followings, and their public-relations men) are no longer
what they were.

"You must go to that ashram near Poona," the Parsi lady, back for a holiday from Europe, said at lunch one day in Bombay. "They say you get a nice mix of East and West there."

The young man who had been described to me as a "minor magnate" said with unexpected passion: "It's a terrible place. It's full of American women who go there to debauch."

There was a risen-dough quality about the magnate's face and physique which hinted at a man given to solitary sexual excitations. He said he was "one of the last, decaying capitalists"; he liked "fleshly comforts." Ashram life wasn't for him; it was possible to make money more easily in India than in any other country, barring the Arab sheik-doms. "Sometimes at night I think about giving it all up. And then in the morning, when I think about speculations and manipulations, I wonder, what's the use of it all? Why stop?"

It was only half a joke. There are times now when India appears able to parody the old idea of itself.

Parody; and sometimes unconscious mimicry. In September 1975 this letter was featured in, of all places, the *Economic Times* of New Delhi:

Man doesn't realize his real purpose on earth so long as he rolls in comforts. . . . It's absolutely true that adversity teaches a man a bitter lesson, toughens his fibre and moulds his character. In other words, an altogether new man is born out of adversity which helpfully destroys one's ego and makes one humble and selfless. . . . Prolonged suffering opens the eyes to hate the things for which one craved before un-duly, leading eventually even to a state of resignation. It then dawns on us that continued yearning brings us intense agony. . . . But the stoic mind is least perturbed by the vicissitudes of life. It's well within our efforts to conquer grief. It's simple. Develop an attitude of detachment even while remaining in the thick of terrestrial pleasures.

In a financial newspaper! But India is India; and the letter seems at first quite Indian, a statement of the Hindu-Buddhist ideal of nonattachment. But the writer has got there by a tortured Western route. Much of his language is borrowed; and his attitude isn't as Hindu or Buddhist as it seems. The image of the smiling Buddha is well known. He has the bump of developed consciousness on his head, the very long ears of comprehension, the folds of wisdom down his neck. But these iconographic distortions do not take away from his humanity. His lips are full, his cheeks round, and he has a double chin. His senses haven't atrophied (the Buddha tried and rejected the ascetic way); he is at peace with the senses. The possession of the senses is part of his serenity, part of his wholeness, and the very basis of the continuing appeal of this image after two thousand years. It isn't nonattachment like this that the letter-writer proposes, but something quite different, more Western: stoicism, resignation, with more than a touch of bitterness: a consumer's lament.

" 'Why do you blame the country for everything? It has been good enough for four hundred millions,' Jagan said, remembering the heritage of *Ramayana* and *Bhagavad Gita* and all the trials and sufferings he had undergone to win independence."

This outburst is from *The Vendor of Sweets*. And for too long this self-satisfaction—expressed in varying ways, and most usually in meaningless exhortations to return to the true religion, and laments for Gandhianism: mechanical turns of the prayer wheel—has passed in India for thought. But Gandhianism has had its great day; and the simple assertion of Indian antiquity won't do now. The heritage is there, and will always be India's; but it can be seen now to belong to the past, to be part of the classical world. And the heritage has oppressed: Hinduism hasn't been good enough for the millions. It has exposed us to a thousand years of defeat and stagnation. It has given men no idea of a contract with other men, no idea of the state. It has enslaved one quarter of the population and always left the whole fragmented and vulnerable. Its philosophy of withdrawal has diminished men intellectually and not equipped them to respond to challenge; it has stifled growth. So that again and again in India history has repeated itself: vulnerability, defeat, withdrawal. And there are not four hundred millions now, but something nearer seven hundred.

The unregarded millions have multiplied and now, flooding into the cities, cannot be denied. The illegal hutments in which they live are knocked down; but they rise again, a daily tide wrack on the margin of cities and beside the railway lines and the industrial highways. It was this new nearness of the millions, this unknown India on the move, together with the triviality of Indian thought on most subjects—the intellectual deficiencies of the archaic civilization finally revealed during this Emergency, India stalled, unable to see its way ahead, to absorb and render creative the changes it has at last generated—it was this great uncertainty, this sense of elemental movement from below, and an almost superstitious dread of this land of impressive, unfinished ruins, that made the professional man say in Delhi: "It's terrible to see your life's work turning to ashes." And his wife said, "For the middle classes, for people who live like us, it's all over. We have a sense of doom."

Part Two

A NEW CLAIM
ON THE LAND

3

The Skyscrapers
and the Chawls

1

It is said that every day 1,500 more people, about 350 families, arrive in Bombay to live. They come mainly from the countryside and they have very little; and in Bombay there isn't room for them. There is hardly room for the people already there. The older apartment blocks are full; the new skyscrapers are full; the small, low huts of the squatters' settlements on the airport road are packed tightly together. Bombay shows its overcrowding. It is built on an island, and its development has been haphazard. Outside the defense area at the southern tip of the island, open spaces are few; cramped living quarters and the heat drive people out into such public areas as exist, usually the streets; so that to be in Bombay is always to be in a crowd. By day the streets are clogged; at night the pavements are full of sleepers.

From late afternoon until dinnertime, on the ground floor of the Taj Mahal Hotel, which now extends over a city block, the middle class and the stylish (but hardly rich, and certainly not as rich as the foreign tourists) promenade past the hotel shops and restaurants in the mild, air-conditioned air: an elegant, sheltered bustle, separated by the hotel carport, the fierce Sikh or Gurkha doormen, the road and the parked cars, from the denser swirl of the white-clad crowd around the Gateway of India, the air moist, the polluted Arabian Sea slapping against the stone steps, the rats below the Gateway not furtive, mingling easily with the crowd, and at nightfall as playful as baby rabbits.

Sometimes, on festive days, stripped divers, small and bony, sit or stand on the sea wall, waiting to be asked to dive into the oily water. Sometimes there is a little band—Indian drums, Western trumpets—attached to some private religious ceremony. Night deepens; the ships' lights in the harbor grow brighter; the Taj Mahal lobby glitters behind its glass wall. The white crowd—with the occasional red or green or yellow of a sari—melts away; and then around the Gateway and the hotel only the sleepers and the beggars remain, enough at any time for a quick crowd, in this area where hotels and dimly lit apartment buildings and stores and offices and small factories press against one another, and where the warm air, despite the sea, always feels overbreathed.

The poor are needed as hands, as labor; but the city was not built to accommodate them. One report says that 100,000 people sleep on the pavements of Bombay; but this figure seems low. And the beggars: are there only 20,000 in Bombay, as one newspaper article says, or are there 70,000, the figure given on another day?

Whatever the number, it is now felt that there are too many. The very idea of beggary, precious to Hindus as religious theater, a demonstration of the workings of *karma*, a reminder of one's duty to oneself and one's future lives, has been devalued. And the Bombay beggar, displaying his unusual mutilations (inflicted in childhood by the beggar-master who had acquired him, as proof of the young beggar's sins in a previous life), now finds, unfairly, that he provokes annoyance rather than awe. The beggars themselves, forgetting their Hindu function, also pester tourists; and the tourists misinterpret the whole business, seeing in the beggary of the few the beggary of all. The beggars have become a nuisance and a disgrace. By becoming too numerous they have lost their place in the Hindu system and have no claim on anyone.

The poet in Vijay Tendulkar's 1972 play *The Vultures* rebukes his tender-hearted sister-in-law for bringing him tea "on the sly, like alms to a beggar." And she replies, hurt, "There wasn't any shortage of beggars at our door that I should bring it as alms to you." But already that ritualistic attitude to beggary seems to belong to a calmer world. There is talk in Bombay of rounding up all the beggars, of impounding them, expelling them, dumping them out of sight somewhere, keeping them out. There is more: there is talk among high and low of declaring the city closed, of issuing work permits, of keeping out new arrivals. Bombay, like all the other big Indian cities, has at last begun to feel itself under siege.

The talk of work permits and barriers at the city boundaries is impractical and is known to be impractical. It is only an expression of frenzy and helplessness: the poor already possess, and corrupt, the city. The Indian-Victorian-Gothic city with its inherited British public buildings and institutions—the Gymkhana with its wide veranda and spacious cricket ground, the London-style leather-chaired Ripon Club for elderly Parsi gentlemen (a portrait of Queen Victoria as a youngish Widow of Windsor still hanging in the secretary's office)—the city was not built for the poor, the millions. But a glance at the city map shows that there was a time when they were invited in.

In the center of the island on which Bombay is built there is a large area marked "MILLS MILLS MILLS" and "*chawls chawls chawls.*" The mills needed, and need, workers; and the workers live or are accommodated in these chawls. These textile mills—many of them now with antiquated machinery—should have been moved long ago. Bombay might then have been allowed to breathe. But the readily available crowds of the mill area serve every kind of commercial and political interest; and the mills will stay.

Some time ago there was talk of a "twin city" on the mainland, to draw industry and people out of Bombay. The plan fell through. Instead, at the southern tip of the island, on expensively reclaimed land, there sprang up a monstrous development of residential skyscrapers: unimaginative walls of concrete in an unlandscaped desert with, already, on the unmade roads the huts and stalls of the poor, sucked in by the new development. "Here you are . . . QUEEN FOR YOUR STAY," says the most recent *Bombay Handbook*, published by the American Women's Association. "Your dream of having servants is about to come true." There isn't accommodation for the poor; but they are always needed, and forever called in, even now.

So, though every day more corrupted by its poor, Bombay, with the metropolitan glamour of its skyscrapers, appears to boom, and at night especially, from the sea road, is dramatic: towers of light around the central nightmare of the mill area.

The main roads there are wide, wet-black and clean in the middle from traffic, earth-colored at the edges where pavement life flows over onto the road, as it does even on a relaxed Sunday morning, before the true heat and glare, and before the traffic builds up and the hot air turns gritty from the brown smoke of the double-decker buses: already a feeling of the crowd, of busy slender legs, of an immense human stirring behind the tattered commercial façades one sees and in the back streets one doesn't see, people coming out into the open, seeking space.

The area seems at first to be one that has gone down in the world. The commercial buildings are large and have style; but, for all the Indian ornamentation of their façades —the rising sun, the Indo-Aryan swastika for good luck, the Sanskrit character *Om* for holiness—these buildings were built to be what they are, to serve the population they serve. Like the chawls themselves, which in some streets can look like the solid town mansions of a less nervous time, but are newer than they look, many built in the 1930s and 1940s, and built even at that late date as chawls, substandard accommodation for factory labor, one room per family, the urban equivalent of plantation barracks or "ranges," the equivalent, in twentieth-century Bombay, of early industrial England's back-to-back workers' terraces.

The chawl blocks are four or five stories high, and the plan is the same on each floor: single rooms opening onto a central corridor, at the back end of which are lavatories and "facilities." Indian families ramify, and there might be eight people in a room; and "corners" might be rented out, as in Dostoevsky's St. Petersburg, or floor space; or people might sleep in shifts. A chawl room is only a base; chawl life is lived in the open, in the areas between chawls, on the pavements, in the streets. An equivalent crowd in a colder climate might be less oppressive, might be more dispersed and shut away. But this Bombay crowd never quite disperses.

The chawls, however, are provided with facilities. To be an inhabitant of a chawl is to be established. But in the nooks and crannies of this area there is—as always in India —yet another, lower human level, where the people for whom there is no room have made room for themselves. They have founded squatters' settlements, colonies of the dispossessed. And, like the chawl dwellers, they have done more: within the past ten years, out of bits and pieces of a past simplified to legend, and out of the crumbling Hindu system, they have evolved what is in effect a new religion, and they have declared themselves affiliated to an "army," the Shiv Sena, the army of Shiva. Not Shiva the god, but Shivaji the seventeenth-century Maratha guerrilla leader, who challenged the Mughal empire and made the Marathas, the people of the Bombay region, a power in India for a century.

The power of the Marathas was mainly destructive, part of the eighteenth-century Indian chaos that gave Britain an easy empire. But in Bombay the matter is beyond discussion. Shivaji is now deified; he is the unlikely warrior god of the chawls. His cult, as expressed in the Shiv Sena, transmutes a dream of martial glory into a feeling of belonging, gives the unaccommodated some idea of human possibility. And, through the Shiv Sena, it has brought a kind of power. The newly erected equestrian statue that stands outside the Taj Mahal Hotel and looks past the Gateway of India to the sea is of Shivaji. It is an emblem of the power of the Sena, the power of the chawls and pavements and squatters' colonies, the inhabitants of the streets who—until the declaration of the Emergency—had begun to rule the streets. All shop signs in Bombay, if not in two languages now, carry transliterations in the Indian *nagari* script of their English names or styles. That happened overnight, when the Sena gave the word; and the Sena's word was more effective than any government decree.

The Sena "army" is xenophobic. It says that Maharashtra, the land of the Marathas, is for the Maharashtrians. It has won a concession from the government that eighty percent of all jobs shall be held by Maharashtrians. The government feels that anyone who has lived in Bombay or Maharashtra for fifteen years ought to be considered a Maharashtrian. But the Sena says no: a Maharashtrian is someone born of Maharashtrian parents. Because of its xenophobia, its persecution in its early days of South Indian settlers in Bombay, and because of the theatricality of its leader, a failed cartoonist, who is said to admire Hitler, the Sena is often described as "fascist."

But this is an easy, imported word. The Shiv Sena has its own Indian antecedents. In this part of India, in the early, pre-Gandhi days of the Independence movement, there was a cult of Shivaji. After Independence, among the untouchables, there were mass conversions to Buddhism. The assertion of pride, a contracting out, a regrouping: it is the pattern of such movements among the dispossessed or humiliated.

The Shiv Sena, as it is today, is of India, independent India, and it is of industrial Bombay. The Sena, like other recent movements in India, though more positive than most—infinitely more positive, for instance, than the Anand Marg, The Way of Peace, now banned, which preached caste, Hindu spirituality, and power through violence, all of this mingled with ritual murder and mutilation and with homosexuality (recruits desired by the leader were persuaded that they had been girls in previous lives)—the Sena is a great contracting out, not from India, but from a Hindu system, which, in the conditions of today, in the conditions of industrial Bombay, has at last been felt to be inadequate. It is in part a reworking of the Hindu system. Men do not accept chaos; they ceaselessly seek to remake their world; they reach out for such ideas as are accessible and fit their need.

We were going that Sunday morning to a squatters' settlement in the chawl area. We got out of the car at a certain stage, and continued by bus. I was lucky in my guide. He was a rare man in India, much more than the engineer he was by profession. His technical skills went with the graces of an old civilization, with a philosophical turn of mind, a clear-sighted and never sentimental concern about the condition of his country, a wholehearted and un-Indian acceptance of men as men.

But he was an engineer, and practical: he offered no visions of Bombay remade, of the chawls and shanty towns pulled down and the workers acceptably rehoused. India simply didn't have the resources. Its urban future had already arrived, and was there, in the shanty towns, in those spontaneous communities. All that authority could add were services, ameliorative regulation, security. The shanty towns might, in effect, be planned. It was only in this way that the urban poor could be accommodated. But the idea that the poor should be accommodated at all was not yet fully accepted in Bombay. A plan to give the poor thirty-square-yard building plots in the projected twin city had run into opposition from middle-class people who had objected on social grounds—they didn't want the poor too near—and on moral grounds—the poor would sell the plots *at a profit* and, after this immorality of profit, live where they had always lived, in the streets.

The engineer was a Bombay man, but not a man of Maharashtra, and therefore hardly a supporter of the Shiv Sena. It was his interest in housing for the urban poor that had sent him to live for a week or so among the squatters of the mill area, queuing up with them every morning to get his water and to use the latrines. He had discovered a number of simple but important things. Communal washing areas were necessary: women spent a lot of time washing clothes (perhaps because they had so few). Private latrines were impossible; communal latrines (which might be provided by the municipality) would bring about an immediate improvement in sanitation, though children might always have to use the open.

But the most important discovery was the extent and nature of the Shiv Sena's control. A squatters' settlement, a low huddle of mud and tin and tile and old boards, might suggest a random drift of human debris in a vacant city space; but the chances now were that it would be tightly organized. The settlement in which the engineer had stayed, and where we were going that morning, was full of Sena "committees," and these committees were dedicated as much to municipal self-regulation as to the Sena's politics: industrial workers beginning to apply something of the discipline of the factory floor to the areas where they lived.

The middle-class leadership of the Sena might talk of

martial glory and dream of political power. But at this lower and more desperate level the Sena had become something else: a yearning for community, an ideal of self-help, men rejecting rejection. "I love the municipal life." Gandhi had said that in the early days; but municipal self-discipline was one of those Gandhian themes that India hadn't been able to relate to religion or the Independence movement, and hadn't therefore required. It was the Sena now that had, as it were, ritualized the municipal need, which Independence, the industrial revolution, and the pressures of population had made urgent.

The bus stopped, and we were just outside the settlement. It was built on a small, rocky hill above a cemetery, which was green with the monsoon; in the distance were the white skyscrapers of southern Bombay. The narrow entrance lane was flanked by latrine blocks and washing sheds. The latrine blocks were doorless, with a central white-tiled runnel on the concrete floor. They were new, the engineer said: the local Shiv Sena municipal councilor had clearly been getting things done. In one of the washing sheds children were bathing; in the other, women and girls were washing clothes.

The entrance lane was deliberately narrow, to keep out carts and cars. And, within, space was suddenly scarce. The structures were low, very low, little doors opening into tiny, dark, single rooms, every other structure apparently a shop, sometimes a glimpse of someone on a string bed on the earth floor. Men and their needs had shrunk. But the lane was paved, with concrete gutters on either side; without that paving—which was also new—the lane, twisting down the hillside, would have remained an excremental ravine. And the lane and the gutters this Sunday morning looked clean. Much depended, the engineer said, on the "zeal" of the municipal sweeper. Caste here! The pariahs of the pariahs: yet another, lower human level, hidden away somewhere!

There were eight Shiv Sena committee rooms in the settlement. The one we went to was on the main lane. It was a stuffy little shed with a corrugated-iron roof; but the floor, which the engineer remembered as being of earth, was now of concrete; and the walls, formerly of plain brick, had been plastered and whitewashed. There was one portrait. And, interestingly, it was not of the leader of the Shiv Sena or of Shivaji, the Sena's warrior god, but of the long-dead Dr. Ambedkar, the Maharashtrian untouchable leader, law minister in the first government of independent India, the framer of India's now suspended constitution. Popular—and near-ecstatic—movements like the Shiv Sena ritualize many different needs. The Sena here, honoring an angry and (for all his eminence) defeated man, seemed quite different from the Sena the newspapers wrote about.

The members of the committee were all young, in their twenties. The older people, they said, were not interested, and had to be forgotten. But more noticeable, and more moving, than the youth of the committee members was their physical size. They were all so small; their average height was about five feet. Generations of undernourishment had whittled away bodies and muscle (though one man, perhaps from the nature of his manual work, had fairly well-developed arm and back muscles).

The leader was coarse-featured and dark, almost black. He worked in Air India as a technician, and he was in his Sunday clothes. His gray trousers were nicely creased, and a white shirt in a synthetic material shone over the beginnings of a little paunch of respectability. After greeting us he immediately in the Indian way offered hospitality, whispering to an aide about "cola." And presently—no doubt from one of the little shops—two warm bottles of the cola came. There was more whispering, and a little later two tumblers decorated with red arabesques appeared, snatched perhaps from somebody's room.

It was a chemically treated substance, the cola, calling for analysis rather than consumption. But consumption was not required. The first sip had completed the formalities; and soon we were out, walking up the lanes, understanding the Lilliputian completeness of the settlement (even a hand-operated printing machine in one of the shacks, turning out cinema handbills), every now and then coming out into the open, at the edge of the hillside, looking down at the roofs of rusting tin or red Mangalore clay tiles we had left below, beside the graveyard, and looking across to the remote skyscrapers, getting paler in the increasing heat.

The technician, the committee leader, had been living in Bombay for fifteen years and in the squatters' settlement for twelve. He had come as a boy from the countryside and had at first stayed with someone whom he knew; and that only meant, though he didn't say, that he might have had floor space in somebody's room. He had found a small job somewhere and had gone to night school and "matriculated." Getting into Air India afterward as an office boy had been his big break. That airline is the least bureaucratized of Indian organizations: the ambitious office boy had been encouraged to become a technical apprentice.

This almost Victorian tale of self-help and success unfolded as we walked. But self-help of this sort was possible only in the industrial city, whatever its horrors. The technician, if he had stayed behind in his village, might have been nothing, without caste or skill or land, an occasional day laborer, perhaps bound to a master. Now, Air India and the Shiv Sena between them gave him energy and purpose. He said he had no personal ambitions; he wasn't planning to move out of the settlement. And he added, with the first touch of rhetoric, but perhaps also with truth, that he wanted to "serve the people." Look, here was something we should notice: the committees had placed dustbins in the lanes. And he lifted a lid or two to show that the dustbins were being used.

But the shanty town was a shanty town. Dustbins were only dustbins; the latrine blocks and the washing sheds were now not near. The twisting lanes continued, shutting out air, concentrating heat, and the small hillside, its Lilliputian novelty vanished, began to feel like a vast wasps' nest of little dark rooms, often no more than boxes, often with just a bed on the earth floor, sometimes with little black runnels of filth between the rooms, occasional enfeebled rats struggling up the gutters, slimy where steep, scum quickly forming around impediments of garbage.

It was Sunday, the technician said: the municipal sweepers hadn't been. Again! Sweepers, the lowest of the low: their very existence, and their acceptance of their function, the especial curse of India, reinforcing the Indian conviction, even here, and in spite of the portrait of Dr. Ambedkar in the committee room now far below, that it was unclean to clean, and leading to the horrors we were about to come upon.

There were eight committees, and it had at first seemed too many for that small settlement. But eight were apparently not enough. There were some sections of the settlement where for various reasons—perhaps internal political reasons, perhaps a clash of personalities, or perhaps simply an absence of concerned young men—there were as yet no committees. Through these sections we walked without speaking, picking our way between squirts and butts and twists of human excrement. It was unclean to clean; it was unclean even to notice. It was the business of the sweepers to remove excrement, and until the sweepers came, people were content to live in the midst of their own excrement.

Every open space was a latrine; and in one such space we came, suddenly, upon a hellish vision. Two starved Bombay street cows had been tethered there, churning up human excrement with their own; and now, out of this bog, they were being pulled away by two starved women, to neighborhood shouts, the encouraging shouts of a crowd gathering around this scene of isolated, feeble frenzy, theater in the round on an excremental stage, the frightened cows and frantic starveling women (naked skin and bone below their disordered, tainted saris) sinking with every step and tug. The keeping of cows was illegal here, and an inspector of some sort was reported to be coming. A recurring drama: the cows—illegal, but the only livelihood of the women who kept them—had often to be hidden; and they were going to be hidden now, if they could be got away in time, in the rooms where the women lived.

The lane twisted; the scene was left behind. We were going down the other side of the hill now, and were soon in an area where a committee ruled. We passed through an open space, a little square. The committees were determined to keep these open areas, the technician said; but that required vigilance. A squatter's hut could go up overnight, and it was hard then—since all the huts were illegal

—to have just that one pulled down. Once, when the technician was out of the settlement for only three days, a small open area had been built over. They had petitioned to have the new structure pulled down; but the offender had pleaded with the committees, and in the end, for compassionate reasons, they had allowed the structure to stand.

We were now back where we had started, at the foot of the hill, at the entrance, with the washing sheds full of women and girls, and the latrine blocks full of children: slum life from the outside, from the wide main road, but, approached from the other side, like a scene of pastoral, and evidence of what was possible.

The Sena men walked with us to the bus stop. From there the hill, variously roofed, and seemingly roofed all the way down, looked small again. The settlement was full, the technician said. They admitted no newcomers now. Sometimes, but rarely, someone left, and his hut could then be sold to an outsider. The current price would be about four thousand rupees, four hundred dollars. That was high, but the area was central and the settlement was provided with services.

The noon sun hurt; the empty Sunday road shimmered. The bus seemed a long time coming; but at last, trailing a hot brown fog, it came, a red Bombay double-decker, the lower part of its metal sides oily and dust-blown, with deep horizontal scratches, and oddly battered, like foil that had been crumpled and smoothed out.

Back through the chawls then, our red bus mingling with more and more of its fuming fellows, the main roads black and the pavements alive, the cinema posters offering fantasies of plump women and snowy Himalayan peaks, the cluttered, sunlit facades of commercial buildings hung with many brilliant signboards, past the mills and the chimneys, along the fast city highways with the more metropolitan advertisements ("butter at its buttermost") to the skyscrapers and the sea: the Bombay of the white towers, seen from that hillside, which already seemed far away.

2

At dinner that evening—high up in one of those towers —a journalist, speaking frenetically of many things (he was unwilling to write while the censorship lasted, and it all came out in talk), touched the subject of identity. "Indian" was a word that was now without a meaning, he said. He himself—he was in his thirties, of the post-Independence generation—no longer knew what he was; he no longer knew the Hindu gods. His grandmother, visiting Khajuraho or some other famous temple, would immediately be in tune with what she saw; she wouldn't need to be told about the significance of the carvings. He was like a tourist; he saw only an architectural monument. He had lost the key to a whole world of belief and feeling, and was cut off from his past.

At first, and especially after my excursion of the morn-ing, this talk of identity seemed fanciful and narcissistic. Bombay, after all, was Bombay; every man knew how and why he had got there and where he had come from. But then I felt I had misjudged the journalist. He was not speaking fancifully; his passion was real.

Once upon a time, the journalist said, cutting through the dinner-table cross-talk—one woman, apropos of noth-ing, mentioning Flaubert only to dismiss him as a writer of no importance; a dazed advertising man, young but nicely bellied, coming to life to wonder, also apropos of nothing, whether the temperate delights of Kashmir couldn't be "sold" to the sun-parched Arabs of the Persian Gulf— once upon a time, the journalist said, the Indian village was self-sufficient and well ordered. The bull drew the plough and the cow gave milk and the manure of these animals enriched the fields, and the stalks of the abundant harvest fed the animals and thatched the village huts. That was the good time. But self-sufficiency hadn't lasted, because after a while there were too many people. "It isn't an easy thing to say," the journalist said, "but this is where kindness to the individual can be cruelty to the race."

It explained his frenzy. His idea of India was one in which India couldn't be accommodated. It was an idea of India which, for all its seeming largeness, only answered a personal need: the need, in spite of the mess of India, to be Indian, to belong to an established country with an established past. And the journalist was insecure. As an Indian he was not yet secure enough to think of Indian identity as something dynamic, something that could incorporate the millions on the move, the corrupters of the cities.

For the journalist—though he was an economist and had traveled, and was professionally concerned with development and change—Indian identity was not something developing or changing but something fixed, an idealization of his own background, the past he felt he had just lost. Identity was related to a set of beliefs and rituals, a knowledge of the gods, a code, an entire civilization. The loss of the past meant the loss of that civilization, the loss of a fundamental idea of India, and the loss therefore, to a nationalist-minded man, of a motive for action. It was part of the feeling of purposelessness of which many Indians spoke, part of the longing for Gandhian days, when the idea of India was real and seemed full of promise, and the "moral issues" clear.

But it was a middle-class burden, the burden of those whose nationalism—after the years of subjection—required them to have an idea of India. Lower down, in the chawls and the squatters' settlements of the city, among the dispossessed, needs were more elemental: food, shelter, water, a latrine. Identity there was no problem; it was a discovery. Identity was what the young men of the Sena were reaching out to, with the simplicities of their politics and their hero figures (the seventeenth-century Shivaji, warrior chieftain turned to war god, the twentieth-century Dr. Ambedkar, untouchable now only in his sanctity). For the Sena men, and the people they led, the world was new; they saw themselves at the beginning of things: unaccommodated men making a claim on their land for the first time, and out of chaos evolving their own philosophy of community and self-help. For them the past was dead; they had left it behind in the villages.

And every day, in the city, their numbers grew. Every day they came from the villages, this unknown, unacknowledged India, though Bombay was full and many squatters' settlements, like the one on the hill above the graveyard, had been declared closed.

4

The House of Grain

1

The engineer who had introduced me to the squatters'
settlement in Bombay was also working on a cooperative
irrigation scheme up on the Deccan plateau, some miles
southeast of Poona. In India, where nearly everything waits
for the government, a private scheme like this, started by
farmers on their own, was new and encouraging; and one
week I went with the engineer to look.

I joined him at Poona, traveling there from Bombay
by the early morning train, the businessman's train, known
as the Deccan Queen. There was no air-conditioned car-
riage; but on this rainy monsoon morning there was no
Indian dust to keep out. Few of the ceiling fans were on;
and it was soon necessary to slide down the aluminum-
framed window against the chill. Rain and mist over the
mainland sprawl of Greater Bombay; swamp and fresh
green grass in a land apparently returning to wilderness;
occasional factory chimneys and scattered apartment blocks

black and seeming to rot with damp; the shanty towns beside the railway sodden, mud walls and gray thatch seemingly about to melt into the mud and brown puddles of unpaved lanes, the naked electric bulbs of tea stalls alone promising a kind of morning cheer.

But then Bombay faded. And swamp was swamp until the land became broken and, in the hollows, patches of swamp were dammed into irregular little ricefields. The land became bare and rose in smooth rounded hills to the plateau, black boulders showing through the thin covering of monsoon green, the fine grass that grows within three days of the first rain and gives these stony and treeless *ghats* the appearance of temperate parkland.

It doesn't show from the train, but the Bombay-Poona region is one of the most industrialized in India. Poona, at the top of the *ghats*, on the edge of the plateau, is still the military town it was in the British days and in the days of the Maratha glory before that, still the green and leafy holiday town for people who want to get away from the humidity of the Bombay coastland. But it is also, and not at all oppressively, an expanding industrial center. Ordered industrial estates spread over what, just thirteen years ago, when I first saw it, was arid waste land. On these estates there has been some reforestation; and it is said that the rainfall has improved.

The plateau around Poona is now in parts like a new country, a new continent. It provides uncluttered space, and space is what the factory-builders and the machine-makers say they need; they say they are building for the twenty-first century. Their confidence, in the general doubt, is staggering. But it is so in India: the doers are always enthusiastic. And industrial India is a world away from the

India of bureaucrats and journalists and theoreticians. The men who make and use machines—and the Indian industrial revolution is increasingly Indian: more and more of the machines are made in India—glory in their new skills. Industry in India is not what industry is said to be in other parts of the world. It has its horrors; but, in spite of Gandhi, it does not—in the context of India—dehumanize. An industrial job in India is more than just a job. Men handling new machines, exercising technical skills that to them are new, can also discover themselves as men, as individuals.

They are the lucky few. Not many can be rescued from the nullity of the labor of preindustrial India, where there are so many hands and so few tools, where a single task can be split into minute portions and labor can turn to absurdity. The street-sweeper in Jaipur City uses his fingers alone to lift dust from the street into his cart (the dust blowing away in the process, returning to the street). The woman brushing the causeway of the great dam in Rajasthan before the top layer of concrete is put on uses a tiny strip of rag held between her thumb and middle finger. Veiled, squatting, almost motionless, but present, earning her half-rupee, her five cents, she does with her finger dabs in a day what a child can do with a single push of a long-handled broom. She is not expected to do more; she is hardly a person. Old India requires few tools, few skills, and many hands.

And old India lay not far from the glitter of new Poona. The wide highway wound through the soft, monsoon-green land. Bangalore was five hundred miles to the south; but the village where we were going was only a few hours away. The land there was less green, more yellow and brown, showing its rockiness. The monsoon had been prolonged, but the water had run off into lakes. It was from one such lake that water was to be lifted and pumped up to the fields. The water pipe was to be buried four feet in the ground, not to hamper cultivation of the land when it was irrigated, and to lessen evaporation. Already, early in the morning, the heat of the day still to come—and even in this season of rain, the sky full of clouds, the distant hills cool and blue above the gray lake—heat waves were rising off the rocks.

The nationalized agricultural bank had lent the farmers ninety percent of the cost of the project. Ten percent the farmers had to pay themselves, in the form of labor; and the engineer had computed that labor at a hundred feet of pipe trench per farmer. The line of the trench had already been marked; and in the middle of what looked like waste land, the rocks baking in spite of the stiff wind, in the middle of a vast view dipping down to the lake, a farmer with his wife and son was digging his section of the trench.

The man was small and slightly built. He was troubled by his chest and obviously weary. He managed the pickaxe with difficulty; it didn't go deep, and he often stopped to rest. His wife, in a short green sari, squatted on the stony ground, as though offering encouragement by her presence; from time to time, but not often, she pulled out with a mattock those stones the man had loosened; and the white-capped boy stood by the woman, doing nothing. Like a painting by Millet of solitary brute labor, but in an emptier and less fruitful land.

A picture of the pain of old India, it might have seemed. But it contained so much that was new: the local agricultural enthusiast who by his example had encouraged the farmers to think of irrigation and better crops, the idea of self-help that was behind the cooperative, the bank that had advanced the money, the engineer with the social conscience who had thought the small scheme worth his while and every week made the long journey from Bombay to superintend, advise, and listen. It wasn't easy to get qualified men to come out from the city and stay with the project, the engineer said; he had had to recruit and train local assistants.

The digging of the trench had begun the week before. To mark the occasion, they had planted a tree, not far from a temple—three hundred years old, the villagers said —on the top of a hill of rock. The pillars of the temple portico were roughly hewn; the three-domed lantern roof was built up with heavy, roughly dressed slabs of stone. On this plateau of rock the buildings were of stone. Stone was the material people handled with instinctive, casual skill; and the village looked settled and solid and many times built over. In the barrenness of the plateau it was like a living historical site. Old, even ancient architectural conventions—like the lantern roof of the temple—mingled with the new; unrelated fragments of old decorated stone could be seen in walls.

Four lanes met in the irregularly shaped main square. A temple filled each of two corners: and, slightly to one side in the open space of the square, there was a tree on a circular stone-walled platform. People waiting for the morning bus—luxury!—sat or squatted on the wall below the tree and on the stone steps that edged the open raised forecourt of one temple. On this forecourt there was a single pillar, obviously old, with a number of bracket-like projections, like a cactus in stone. It was a common feature of temples in Maharashtra, but people here knew as little about its significance as they did elsewhere. Someone said the brackets were for lights; someone else said they were pigeon perches. The pillar simply went with the temple; it was part of the past, inexplicable but necessary.

The post office was of the present: an ocher-colored shed, with a large official board with plain red lettering. On another side of the square a smaller, gaudier signboard hung over a dark little doorway. This was the village restaurant, and the engineer's assistants said it was no longer to be recommended. The restaurateur, anxious to extend his food-and-drink business, had taken to supplying some people in the village with water. People too poor to pay in cash paid in *chapattis*, unleavened bread; and it was these *chapattis* —the debt-cancelers of the very poor, and more stone than bread—that the restaurateur, ambitious but shortsighted, was now offering with his set meals. He had as a result lost the twice-daily custom of all the engineer's assistants. They had begun to cook for themselves in a downstairs room of the irrigation-project office. And a certain amount of un-spoken ill-will now bounced back and forth across the peaceable little square, with every now and then, on either side, the smoke signals of independence and disdain.

The bus came and picked up its passengers, and the dust settled again. At eleven, rather late in the morning, as it seemed, the schoolchildren appeared, the boys in khaki trousers and white shirts, barefooted but with white Gandhi caps, the girls in white blouses and long green skirts. The school was the two-storied *panchayat* or village-council building in one of the lanes off the square, beyond the other temple, which had a wide, smooth, stone-floored veranda, the wooden pillars of the veranda roof resting on

carved stone bases. Everywhere there was carving; everywhere doorways were carved. Outside every door hung a
basket or pot of earth in which the *tulsi* or basil grew,
sacred to Hindus.

Even without the irrigation scheme, improved agriculture had brought money to this village. Many houses were
being renovated or improved. A new roof of red Mangalore
clay tiles in a terraced lane announced a brand-new building. It was a miniature, very narrow, with just two rooms,
one at the front and one at the back, with shelves and
arched niches set in the thick stone walls. A miniature, but
the roof had required a thousand tiles, at one rupee per
tile: a thousand rupees, a hundred dollars for the roof alone.
But that was precisely the fabled sum another man, just a
short walk away, had spent on the carved wooden door of
his new house, which was much bigger and half built
already, the stone walls already rising about the inset shelves
of new wood, the beautifully cut and pointed stone of the
doorway showing off the wooden door, already hung: wood,
in this land of stone, being especially valuable, and carving,
the making of patterns, even in this land of drought and
famine, still considered indispensable.

The engineer had remained behind in his office. My
guide was now the *sarpanch*, the chairman of the village
panchayat or council; and he, understanding that I was
interested in houses, began to lead the way to his own
house.

He was a plump man, the *sarpanch*, noticeably un-
washed and unshaved; but his hair was well oiled. He was
chewing a full red mouthful of betel nut and he wore
correctly grubby clothes, a dingy long-tailed cream-colored
shirt hanging out over dingier green-striped pajamas, slackly

knotted. The grubbiness was studied, and it was correct because any attempt at greater elegance would have been not only unnecessary and wasteful but also impious, a provocation of the gods who had so far played fair with the *sarpanch* and wouldn't have cared to see their man getting above himself.

In the village it was accepted that the *sarpanch* was blessed: he was distrusted, feared, and envied as a prospering racketeer. Some years before, he had collected money for a cooperative irrigation scheme. That money had simply vanished; and there was nothing that anybody could do about it. Since then the *sarpanch*'s power had if anything increased; and people had to be friendly with him, like the dusty little group scrambling after him now. To anyone who could read the signs, the *sarpanch*'s power showed. It showed in that very full mouth of betel nut that made it difficult for him to speak without a gritty spray of red spittle. It showed in his paunch, which was as it were shaded in appropriate places by an extra griminess on his shirt. The long-tailed shirt, the pajama bottom: the seraglio style of dress proclaimed the *sarpanch* a man of leisure, or at any rate a man unconnected with physical labor. He was in fact a shopkeeper; and his shop stood next to his house.

From the lane the two establishments did not appear connected. The shop was small, its little front room and its goods quite exposed. The house, much wider, was blank-fronted, with a low, narrow doorway in the middle. Within was a central courtyard surrounded by a wide, raised, covered veranda. At the back, off the veranda, and always shaded from the sun, were the private rooms. It was surprising, after the dust and featurelessness of the lane: this ordered domestic courtyard, the dramatization of a small space, the sense of antiquity and completeness, of a building perfectly conceived.

It was an ancient style of house, common to many old civilizations; and here—apart from the tiles of the roof and the timber of the veranda pillars—it had been rendered all in stone. The design had been arrived at through the centuries; there was nothing now that could be added. No detail was unconsidered. The veranda floor, its stone flags polished by use, sloped slightly toward the courtyard, so that water could run off easily. At the edge of the courtyard there were metal rings for tethering animals (though it seemed that the *sarpanch* had none). In one corner of the courtyard was the water container, a clay jar set in a solid square of masonry, an arrangement that recalled the tavern counters of Pompeii. Every necessary thing had its place.

A side passage led to a smaller, paved courtyard. This was at the back of the shop, which, according to a notice painted in English on the inside wall, was mortgaged— "hypothecated" was the word used, and it seemed very fierce in the setting—to a bank. And then we were back in the lane.

A man of property, then, a man used to dealing with banks, and, as chairman of the village council, a politician and a kind of official: I thought the *sarpanch* must be the most important man in the village. But there was a grander: the Patel. The *sarpanch* was a shopkeeper, a money man; the Patel was a landowner, the biggest landowner in the village. He owned fifty good acres; and though he didn't own people, the fate of whole families depended on the Patel. And to these people he was, literally, the Master.

To the house of the Patel, then, we went, by sudden public demand, as it seemed, and in equally sudden procession. The engineer was with us again, and there was a crowd, swamping the group around the *sarpanch*, who now, as we walked, appeared to hang back. Perhaps the Patel was in the crowd. It was hard to say. In the rush there had been no introductions, and among the elderly turbaned men, all looking like peasants, men connected with the work of the land, no one particularly stood out.

The house was indeed the grandest in the village. It was on two floors, and painted. Bright paint colored the two peacocks carved over the doorway. The blank front wall was thick. Within that wall (as in some of the houses in Pompeii) stone steps led to the upper story, a gallery repeating the raised veranda around the courtyard at ground level. The floor was of beaten earth, plastered with a mixture of mud and cow dung. To the left as we entered, on the raised veranda, almost a platform, were two pieces of furniture: a bed with an old striped bedspread embroidered with the name of the village in *nagari* characters, and a new sofa of "contemporary" design with naked wooden legs and a covering in a shiny blue synthetic fabric: the Western-style sofa, sitting in the traditional house just like that and making its intended effect, a symbol of wealth and modernity, like the fluorescent light tube above the entrance.

That part of the veranda with the bed and sofa was for receiving visitors. Visitors did not go beyond this to the courtyard unless they were invited to do so. On the raised veranda to the right of the entrance there was no furniture, only four full sacks of grain, an older and truer symbol of wealth in this land of rock and drought. It was a house of

plenty, a house of grain. Grain was spread out to dry in the
sunlit courtyard; and in the open rooms on either side were
wickerwork silos of grain, silos that looked like enormous
baskets, as tall as a man, the wickerwork plastered to keep
out rats, and plastered, like the floor, with mud and cow
dung.

Invited to look around, received now as guests rather
than official visitors, we walked past the grain drying in the
courtyard to the kitchen at the back. The roof sloped low;
after the sunlight of the courtyard it was dark. To the left
a woman was making curds, standing over the high clay
jar and using one of the earliest tools made by civilized
man: a cord double-wound around a pole and pulled on
each end in turn: the carpenter's drill of ancient Egypt,
and also the very churning tool depicted in those eighteenth-
century miniatures from the far north of India that deal
with the frolics of the dark god Krishna among the pale
milkmaids. In the kitchen gloom to the right a *chulha* or
earthen fireplace glowed: to me romantic, but the engineer
said that a simple hinged opening in the roof would get
rid of the smoke and spare the women's eyes.

Our visit wasn't expected, but the kitchen was as clean
and ordered as though for inspection. Brass and silver and
metal vessels glittered on one shelf; tins were neatly ranged
on the shelf below that. And—another sign of modernity,
of the new age—from a nail on the wall a transistor radio
hung by its strap.

The woman or girl at the fireplace rose, fair, well
mannered in the Indian way, and brought her palms
together. She was the Patel's daughter-in-law. And the
Patel (still remaining unknown) was too grand to boast of
her attainments. That he could leave to the others, his

admirers and hangers-on. And the others did pass on the
news about the daughter-in-law of this wealthy man. She
was a graduate! Though lost and modest in the gloom of
the kitchen, stooping over the fire and the smoke, she was
a graduate!

The back door of the kitchen opened onto the back
yard; and we were in the bright sun again, in the dust, at
the edge of the village, the rocky land stretching away. As
so often in India, order, even fussiness, had ended with the
house itself. The back yard was heaped with this and that,
and scattered about with bits and pieces of household
things that had been thrown out but not quite abandoned.
But even here there were things to show. Just a few steps
from the back door was a well, the Patel's own, high-
walled, with a newly concreted base, and with a length
of rope hanging from a weighted pole, a trimmed and
peeled tree branch. A rich man indeed, this Patel, to have
his own well! No need for him to buy water from the
restaurant man and waste grain on *chapattis* no one wanted.
And the Patel had something else no one in the village
had: an outhouse, a latrine! There it was, a safe distance
away. No need for him or any member of his family to
crouch in the open! It was like an extravagance, and we
stood and marveled.

We reentered the house of grain and food and graduate
daughter-in-law—still at her fireplace—and walked back,
around the drying grain in the courtyard, to the front
vestibule. We went up the steps set in the front wall to
the upper story. It was being refloored: interwoven wooden
strips laid on the rafters, mud on that, and on the mud
thin slabs of stone, so that the floor, where finished, though
apparently of stone, was springy.

Little low doors led to a narrow balcony where, in the center, in what was like a recessed shrine, were stone busts, brightly painted, of the Patel's parents. This was really what, as guests, we had been brought up to the unfinished top floor to see. The *nagari* inscription below the busts said that the house was the house of the Patel's mother. The village honored the Patel as a rich man and a Master; he made himself worthy of that reverence, he avoided hubris, and at the same time he made the reverence itself more secure, by passing it backward, as it were, to his ancestors. We all stood before the busts—bright paint flattening the features to caricature—and looked. It was all that was required; by looking we paid homage.

Even now I wasn't sure who, among the elderly men with us, was the Patel. So many people seemed to speak for him, to glory in his glory. As we were going down again, I asked the engineer, "What is the value of this house? Is that a good question to ask?" He said, "It is a very good question to ask." He asked for me. It was a question only the Patel himself could answer.

And the Patel, going down the steps, revealed himself, and his quality, by evading the question. If, he said, speaking over his shoulder, the upper flooring was completed in the way it had been begun—the wood, the mud plaster, the stone slabs—then the cost of that alone would be sixty thousand rupees, six thousand dollars. And then, downstairs, seating us, his guests, on the visitors' platform, on the blue-covered modern sofa and the bed with the embroidered bedspread, he seemed to forget the rest of the question.

Tea was ordered, and it came almost at once. The graduate daughter-in-law in the kitchen at the back knew her duties. It was tea brewed in the Indian way, sugar and tea leaves and water and milk boiled together into a thick stew, hot and sweet. The tea, in chipped china cups, came first for the chief guests. We drank with considered speed, held out our cups to surrender them—the Patel now, calm in his role as host, detaching himself from his zealous attendants—and presently the cups reappeared, washed and full of the milky tea for the lesser men.

And the Patel sat below us, in the vestibule, looking like so many of the villagers, a slight, wrinkled man in a peasant-style turban, a dhoti and koortah and brown woolen scarf, all slightly dingy, but mainly from dust and sweat, and not as studiedly grimed as the *sarpanch*'s shirt and slack pajama bottom. But as he sat there, no longer unknown but a man who had established his worth, our host, the provider of tea (still being slurped at and sighed over), the possessor of this house (was he boasting about the cost of the new floor?), his personality became clearer. The small, twinkly eyes that might at first, in that wrinkled head, have seemed only peasant's eyes, always about to register respect and obsequiousness combined with disbelief, could be seen now to be the eyes of a man used to exercising a special kind of authority, an authority that to him and the people around him was more real, and less phantasmal, than the authority of outsiders from the city. His face was the face of the Master, the man who knew men, and whole families, as servants, from their birth to their death.

He said, talking about the great cost of the new floor (and still evading the question about the value of the house), that he didn't believe in borrowing. Other people believed in borrowing, but he didn't. He did things only when he had the money to do them. If he made money one year, then there were certain things he felt he could do. That had been his principle all his life; that was how he intended to do the new floor, year by year and piece by piece. And yet he—like the *sarpanch*, and perhaps to a greater degree than the *sarpanch*—was almost certainly a moneylender. Many of the people I had seen that morning would have been in debt to the Patel. And in these villages interest rates were so high, ten percent or more a month, that debts, once contracted, could never be repaid. Debt was a fact of life in these villages; interest was a form of tribute.

But it was also true that when the Patel spoke about borrowing he was not being insincere. The occasion was special. We were outsiders; he had done us the honors of his house; and now, in public audience, as it were, he was delivering himself of his proven wisdom. This was the wisdom that lifted him above his fellows; and this was the wisdom that his attendants were acknowledging with beatific smiles and slow, affirmative swings of the head, even while accepting that what was for the Patel couldn't be for them.

Now that we were on the subject of money, and the high cost of things these days, we spoke about electricity. There was that fluorescent tube, slightly askew and in a tangle of cord, in the vestibule: it couldn't be missed. The government had brought electricity to the village five years before, the Patel said; and he thought that forty percent of the village now had electricity. It was interesting that he too had adopted the official habit of speaking in percentages rather than in old-fashioned numbers. But the figure he gave seemed high, because the connection charge was 275 rupees, over twenty-seven dollars, twice a laborer's monthly wage, and electricity was as expensive as in London.

Electricity wasn't for the poor. But electricity hadn't

been brought across the plateau just to light the villages. Its primary purpose was to develop agriculture; without electricity the irrigation scheme wouldn't have been possible. Electricity mattered mainly to the people with land to work. As lighting it was still only a toy. So it was even in the Patel's house. The fluorescent tube in the vestibule, far from the kitchen and the inner rooms off the veranda, was the only electrical fitting in the house. There were still oil lamps about and they were evidently in daily use.

The fluorescent tube, like the shining blue sofa for visitors, was only a garnish, a modern extra. Sixty percent of the village was without electricity, and village life as a whole still took its rhythm from the even length of the tropical day. Twelve hours of darkness followed twelve hours of light; people rose at dawn and retired at dusk; every day, as from time immemorial, darkness fell on the village like a kind of stultification.

The village had had so little, had been left to itself for so long. After two decades of effort and investment simple things had arrived, but were still superfluous to daily life, answered no established needs. Electric light, ready water, an outhouse: the Patel was the only man in the village to possess them all, and only the water would have been considered strictly necessary. Everything else was still half for show, proof of the Patel's position, the extraordinariness which yet, fearing the gods, he took care to hide in his person, in the drabness and anonymity of his peasant appearance.

It was necessary to be in the village, to see the Patel and his attendants, to understand the nature of the power of that simple man, to see how easily such a man could, if he wished, frustrate the talk from Delhi about minimum wages, the abolition of untouchability, the abolition of rural indebtedness. How could the laws be enforced? Who would be the policeman in the village? The Patel was more than the biggest landowner. In that village where needs were still so basic, the Patel, with his house of grain, ruled; and he ruled by custom and consent. In his authority, which in his piety he extended backward to his ancestors, there was almost the weight of religion.

The irrigation scheme was a cooperative project. But the village was not a community of peasant farmers. It was divided into people who had land and people who hadn't; and the people who had land were divided into those who were Masters and those who weren't. The Patel was the greatest Master in the village. The landless laborers he employed (out somewhere in his fields now) were his servants; many had been born his servants. He acknowledged certain obligations to them. He would lend them money so that they could marry off their daughters with appropriate ceremony; in times of distress they knew that they could turn to him; in times of famine they knew they had a claim on the grain in his house. Their debts would wind around them and never end, and would be passed on to their children. But to have a Master was to be in some way secure. To be untied was to run the risk of being lost.

And the Patel was progressive. He was a good farmer. It was improved farming (and the absence of tax on agricultural income) that had made him a rich man. And he welcomed new ways. Not everyone in his position was like that. There were villages, the engineer said later, when we were on the highway again, which couldn't be included in the irrigation scheme because the big landowners there didn't like the idea of a lot of people making more money.

The Patel wasn't like that, and the engineer was careful not to cross him. The engineer knew that he could do nothing in the village without the cooperation of the Patel. As an engineer, he was to help to increase food production; and he kept his ideas about debt and servants and bonded labor to himself.

The countryside was ruled by a network of men like the Patel. They were linked to one another by caste and marriage. The Patel's daughter-in-law—who might not have been absolutely a graduate: she had perhaps simply gone for a few years to a secondary school—would have come from a family like the Patel's in another village. She would have exchanged one big house of grain for another; in spite of her traditional kitchen duties, she would be conscious of her connections. Development had touched people unequally. To some it had given a glimpse of a new world; others it had bound more fast in the old. Development had increased the wealth, and the traditional authority, of the Patel; it had widened the gap between the landed and the landless. Backed up by people like the *sarpanch*, minor politicians, minor officials, courted by administrators and the bigger politicians, men like the Patel now controlled; and nothing could be done without them. In the villages they had become the law.

From the *Times of India*, September 2, 1975:

The Maharashtra chief minister, Mr. S. B. Chavan, admitted in Bombay on Monday that he was aware of big landlords in the rural areas using the local police to drive poor peasants off their land, particularly during the harvest season. Seemingly legal procedures were being used by the police and the landlords to accomplish this purpose, he added.

On the way back to Poona we stopped at the temple of Zezuri, like a Mughal fort, high up on a black hill. Mutilated beggar children—one girl with flesh recently scooped out of a leg—were hurried out to the lower steps and arranged in postures of supplication. Garish little shrines stained saffron and red, and their patient keepers, all the way up to the temple; archway after archway, eighteenth-century ornamented stucco crumbling over brick; bracketed pillars of varying size and age; on the stone steps, the worn carved inscriptions in various scripts of generations of pilgrims. At the top, on the windy parapet, a view through the Mughal arches of the town's two tanks or reservoirs (one collapsed and empty) and the monsoon-green plateau in a clouded sunset.

But the rain that had greened the plateau had also, the next morning, made the outskirts of Poona messy: a line of transport-office shacks and motor-repair shops in yards turned to mud. The busy Poona-Bombay road, badly made, was rutted and broken. In time, going down from the plateau, we came to the smooth, rounded green hills, like parkland, over which rain and shifting mist ceaselessly played: during the monsoon months a holiday landscape to people from the coast, at other times scorched and barren, barely providing pasture for animals. At Lonavala, where we broke our journey, a buffalo herdsman sang in the rain. We heard his song before we saw him, on a hill, driving his animals before him. He was half naked and carried an open black umbrella. When the rain slanted and he held the umbrella at his side, it was hard to tell him from his buffaloes.

But the land, though bare, offering nothing or very little, was never empty. All the way from Poona—except

in certain defense areas—it was dotted with sodden little
clusters of African-like huts: the encampments of people
in flight from the villages, people who had been squeezed
out and had nowhere else to go, except here, near the
highway, close to the towns, exchanging nullity for nullity:
people fleeing not only from landlessness but also from
tyranny, the rule in a thousand villages of men like the
Patel and the *sarpanch*.

2

In some parts of central and northwestern India, men
squeezed out or humiliated can take to the ravines and
gullies and become dacoits, outlaws, brigands. Whole
criminal communities are formed. They are hunted down,
and sometimes a district-police communiqué gets into the
Indian press ("Anti-Dacoit Operation Pays Big Dividends":
Blitz, October 4, 1975). This is traditional; the dacoit
leader and the "dacoit queen" are almost figures of folklore.
But some years ago there was something bigger. Some years
ago, in Bengal in the northeast and Andhra in the south,
there was a tragic attempt at a revolution.

This was the Naxalite movement. The name comes from
Naxalbari, the district in the far north of Bengal where, in
1968, it all began. It wasn't a spontaneous uprising and it
wasn't locally led; it was organized by communists from
outside. Land was seized and landowners were killed. The
shaky, semipopulist government of the state was slow to
act; the police might even have been ambivalent; and
"Naxalism" spread, catching fire especially in large areas of
Andhra in the south. Then the government acted. The
areas of revolt were surrounded and severely policed; and
the movement crumbled.

But the movement lasted long enough to engage the sympathies of young people at the universities. Many gave up their studies and became Naxalites, to the despair of their parents. Many were killed; many are still in jail. And now that the movement is dead, it is mainly in cities that people remember it. They do not talk about it often; but when they do, they speak of it as a middle-class—rather than a peasant—tragedy. One man put it high: he said that in the Naxalite movement India had lost the best of a whole generation, the most educated and idealistic of its young people.

In Naxalbari itself nothing shows and little is remembered. Life continues as before in the green, rich-looking countryside that in places—though the Himalayas are not far away—recalls the tropical lushness of the West Indies. The town is the usual Indian country town, ramshackle and dusty, with its little shops and stalls, its overloaded buses, cycle-rickshaws, carts. It is there, in the choked streets, after the well-tilled and well-watered fields, after the sense of space and of the nearness of the cool mountains, that the overpopulation shows. And yet the land, unusually in India, is not "old." It was forest until the last century, when the British established tea plantations or "gardens" there, and brought in indentured laborers—mainly from far-off aboriginal communities, pre-Aryan people—to work the gardens.

The tea gardens are now Indian-owned, but little has changed. Indian caste attitudes perfectly fit plantation life and the clannishness of the planters' clubs; and the Indian tea men, clubmen now in the midst of the aborigines, have adopted, almost as a sign of caste, and no longer with conscious mimicry, the style of dress of their British predecessors: the shirt, the shorts, and the socks. The tea workers remain illiterate, alcoholic, lost, a medley of tribal people without traditions and now (as in some places in the West Indies) even without a language, still strangers in the land, living not in established villages but (again as in the old plantations of the West Indies) in shacks strung along the estate roads.

There isn't work for everyone. Many are employed only casually; but this possibility of casual labor is enough to keep people tied to the gardens. In the hours of daylight, with panniers on their backs like natural soft carapaces, the employed flit about the level tea bushes, in the shade of tall rain trees (West Indian trees, imported to shade the tea), like a kind of protected wildlife, diligent but timid, sent scuttling by a sudden shower or the factory whistle, but always returning to browse, plucking, plucking at the endless hedging of the tea bushes, gathering in with each nip the two tender leaves and a bud that alone can be fermented and dried into tea. Tea is one of India's most important exports, a steady earner of money; and it might have been expected that the tea workers would have been among the most secure of rural workers. They are among the most depressed and—though the estate people say that they nowadays resent abuse—among the most stultified.

But it wasn't because of the tea workers—that extra level of distress—that the revolutionaries chose Naxalbari. The tea workers were, in fact, left alone. The Naxalbari district was chosen, by men who had read the handbooks of revolution, for its terrain: its remoteness, and the cover provided by its surviving blocks of forest. The movement that began there quickly moved on; it hardly touched the real distress of Naxalbari; and now nothing shows.

The movement is now dead. The reprisals, official and

personal, continue. From time to time in the Indian press there is still an item about the killing or capture of "Naxalites." But social inquiry is outside the Indian tradition; journalism in India has always been considered a gracious form of clerkship; the Indian press—even before the Emergency and censorship—seldom investigated the speeches or communiqués or bald agency items it printed as news. And that word "Naxalite," in an Indian newspaper, can now mean anything.

The communists, or that group of communists concerned with the movement, interpret events in their own way; they have their own vocabulary. Occasionally they circulate reports about the "execution" of "peasant leaders." The Naxalite movement—for all its tactical absurdity—was an attempt at Maoist revolution. But was it a "peasant" movement? Did the revolutionaries succeed in teaching their complex theology to people used to reverencing a Master and used for centuries to the idea of *karma?* Or did they preach something simpler? It was necessary to get men to act violently. Did the revolutionaries then—as a communist journalist told me revolutionaries in India generally should do—preach only the idea of the enemy?

It is the theory of Vijay Tendulkar, the Marathi playwright—who has been investigating this business as someone sympathetic to the Naxalites' stated cause of land reform, as most Indians are sympathetic—it is Tendulkar's theory that Naxalism, as it developed in Bengal, became confused with the Kali cult: Kali, "the black one," the coal-black aboriginal goddess, surviving in Hinduism as the emblem of female destructiveness, garlanded with human skulls, tongue forever out for fresh blood, eternally sacrificed to but insatiable. Many of the Naxalite killings in

Bengal, according to Tendulkar, had a ritualistic quality. Maoism was used only to define the sacrifice. Certain people —not necessarily rich or powerful—might be deemed "class enemies." Initiates would then be bound to the cause—of Kali, of Naxalism—by being made to witness the killing of these class enemies and dipping their hands in the blood.

In the early days, when the movement was far away and appeared revolutionary and full of drama, the Calcutta press published gruesome and detailed accounts of the killings: it was in these repetitive accounts that Tendulkar spotted the ritualism of cult murder. But as the movement drew nearer the city, the press took fright and withdrew its interest. It was as an affair of random murder, the initiates now mainly teenagers, that the movement came to Calcutta, became part of the violence of that cruel city, and then withered away. The good cause—in Bengal, at any rate —had been lost long before in the cult of Kali. The initiates had been reduced to despair, their lives spoiled for good; old India had once again depressed men into barbarism.

But the movement's stated aims had stirred the best young men in India. The best left the universities and went far away, to fight for the landless and the oppressed and for justice. They went to a battle they knew little about. They knew the solutions better than they knew the problems, better than they knew the country. India remains so little known to Indians. People just don't have the information. History and social inquiry, and the habits of analysis that go with these disciplines, are too far outside the Indian tradition. Naxalism was an intellectual tragedy, a tragedy of idealism, ignorance, and mimicry: middle-class India, after the Gandhian upheaval, incapable of generating ideas and institutions of its own, needing constantly in the modern world to be inducted into the art, science, and ideas of other civilizations, not always understanding the consequences, and this time borrowing something deadly, somebody else's idea of revolution.

But the alarm has been sounded. The millions are on the move. Both in the cities and in the villages there is an urgent new claim on the land; and any idea of India which does not take this claim into account is worthless. The poor are no longer the occasion for sentiment or holy alms-giving; land reform is no longer a matter for the religious conscience. Just as Gandhi, toward the end of his life, was isolated from the political movement he had made real, so what until now has passed for politics and leadership in independent India has been left behind by the uncontrollable millions.

Part Three

NOT IDEAS,
BUT OBSESSIONS

5

A Defect of Vision

In 1888, when he was nineteen, and already married for
six years, Gandhi went to England to study law. It was a
brave thing to do. Not the English law—which, however
alien to a Hindu of 1888, however unconnected with his
complicated rites and his practice of magic, could be
mugged up, like another series of *mantras*—not the law,
but the voyage itself. Hindu India, decaying for centuries,
constantly making itself archaic, had closed up; and the
rules of Gandhi's Gujarati merchant caste—at one time
great travelers—now forbade travel to foreign countries.
Foreign countries were polluting to pious Hindus; and no
one of the caste had been to England before.

To please his mother, Gandhi had taken vows not to
touch wine, meat, or women while abroad. But these vows
did not satisfy everybody. One section of the caste formally
declared the young man an outcaste. But Gandhi, though
timid, was obstinate. For a reason which he never makes

clear—he was virtually uneducated, had never even read a newspaper—he passionately wanted to go to England. He began to be afraid that the caste might prevent his going; and, two months earlier than he had planned, he took a ship from Bombay to Southampton.

And this is how, in his autobiography, *The Story of My Experiments with Truth*, written nearly forty years later, when he had become the Mahatma, Gandhi remembers the great adventure (the translation is by his secretary, Mahadev Desai):

> I did not feel at all sea-sick. . . . I was innocent of the use of knives and forks. . . . I therefore never took meals at table but always had them in my cabin, and they consisted principally of sweets and fruits I had brought with me. . . . We entered the Bay of Biscay, but I did not begin to feel the need either of meat or liquor. . . . However, we reached Southampton, as far as I remember, on a Saturday. On the boat I had worn a black suit, the white flannel one, which my friends had got me, having been kept especially for wearing when I landed. I had thought that white clothes would suit me better when I stepped ashore, and therefore I did so in white flannels. Those were the last days of September, and I found I was the only person wearing such clothes.

That is the voyage: an internal adventure of anxieties felt and food eaten, with not a word of anything seen or heard that did not directly affect the physical or mental well-being of the writer. The inward concentration is fierce, the self-absorption complete. Southampton is lost in that embarrassment (and rage) about the white flannels. The name of the port is mentioned once, and that is all, as though the name is description enough. That it was late

September was important only because it was the wrong time of year for white flannels; it is not a note about the weather. Though Gandhi spent three years in England, there is nothing in his autobiography about the climate or the seasons, so unlike the heat and monsoon of Gujarat and Bombay; and the next date he is precise about is the date of his departure.

No London building is described, no street, no room, no crowd, no public conveyance. The London of 1890, capital of the world—which must have been overwhelming to a young man from a small Indian town—has to be inferred from Gandhi's continuing internal disturbances, his embarrassments, his religious self-searchings, his attempts at dressing correctly and learning English manners, and, above all, his difficulties and occasional satisfactions about food.

Sir Edwin Arnold, known for his verse translation of the *Gita,* is mentioned, but only mentioned and never described, though Gandhi must have been dazzled by him, and the poet wasted some time as vice-president of a vegetarian club Gandhi started and ran for a short while in Bayswater. There is an entertaining account of a very brief call, with a visiting Indian writer, on Cardinal Manning. But generally English people are far away in Gandhi's London. There is no reference to plays (an account of a visit to an unnamed theater turns out to be an anecdote about an uneaten dinner). Apart from a sentence about Cardinal Manning and the London dock strike, there is nothing about politics or politicians. The only people who come out of the void and make some faint impression are cranks, Theosophists, proselytizing vegetarians. And though they seem of overwhelming importance (Dr. Oldfield, editor of *The Vegetarian*, "Dr. Allinson of vegetarian fame," Mr. Howard or Mr. Howard Williams, author of *The Ethics of Diet*, Mr. Hills, a puritan and "proprietor of the Thames Iron Works"), they are hardly seen as people or set in interiors. They are only their names, their status (Gandhi is always scrupulous about titles), and their convictions.

And then, quite suddenly, Gandhi is a lawyer; and the adventure of England is over. As anxious as he had been to get to London, so he is now anxious to leave. "I passed my examinations, was called to the bar on the 10th of June 1891, and enrolled in the High Court on the 11th. On the 12th I sailed for home."

And yet, curiously, it was again a wish for travel and adventure that two years later sent Gandhi to South Africa. He went on law business and intended to stay for a year. He stayed for twenty years. England had been unsettling only because it hadn't been India. But in England Gandhi had ceased to be a creature of instinct; out of his unsettlement there, and his consequent self-searching, he had decided that he was a vegetarian and a Hindu by conviction. South Africa offered direct racial hostility; and Gandhi, obstinate as always, was immeasurably fortified as a Hindu and an Indian. It was in South Africa that he became the Mahatma, the great-souled, working through religion to political action as leader of the Indian community, and through political action back to religion. The adventure never ceased to be internal: so it comes out in the autobiography. And this explains the most remarkable omission in Gandhi's account of his twenty active years in South Africa: Africans.

Africans appear only fleetingly at a time of a "rebellion,"

when for six weeks Gandhi led an Indian ambulance unit and found himself looking after wounded Africans. He says his heart was with the Africans; he was distressed by the whippings and unnecessary shootings; it was a trial, he says, to have to live with the soldiers responsible. But the experience did not lead him to a political decision about Africans. He turned inward and, at the age of thirty-seven, did what he had been thinking about for six years: he took the Hindu vow of *brahmacharya*, the vow of lifelong sexual abstinence. And the logic was like this: to serve humanity, as he was then serving the Africans, it was necessary for him to deny himself "the pleasures of family life," to hold himself free in the spirit and the flesh. So the Africans vanish in Gandhi's heart-searchings; they are the motive of a vow, and thereafter disappear.

Far away, at Yasnaya Polyana in Russia, Tolstoy, in the last year of his life, said of Gandhi, whose work he followed and with whom he exchanged letters: "His Hindu nationalism spoils everything." It was a fair comment. Gandhi had called his South African commune Tolstoy Farm; but Tolstoy saw more clearly than Gandhi's English and Jewish associates in South Africa, fellow seekers after the truth. Gandhi really had little to offer these people. His experiments and discoveries and vows answered his own need as a Hindu, the need constantly to define and fortify the self in the midst of hostility; they were not of universal application.

Gandhi's self-absorption was part of his strength. Without it he would have done nothing and might even have been destroyed. But with this self-absorption there was, as always, a kind of blindness. In the autobiography South Africa is inevitably more peopled than England, and more variously peopled; there are more events. But the mode of narration is the same. People continue to be only their names and titles, their actions or convictions, their quality of soul; they are never described and never become individuals. There is no attempt at an objective view of the world. As events pile up, the reader begins to be nagged by the absence of the external world; when the reader ceases to share or follow Gandhi's convictions, he can begin to feel choked.

Landscape is never described. I may be proved wrong, but in all the great length of *My Experiments with Truth* I believe there are only three gratuitous references to landscape. In 1893, on the way out to South Africa, Gandhi notices the vegetation of Zanzibar; three years later, returning briefly to India, he lands at Calcutta, "admiring the beauty" of the Hooghly River. His only important experience of landscape comes at the age of forty-five when, back in India for good, he goes to Hardwar, a place of Hindu pilgrimage in the Himalayas. "I was charmed with the natural scenery about Hrishikesh and Lakshman Jhula, and bowed my head in reverence to our ancestors for their sense of the beautiful in Nature, and their foresight in investing beautiful manifestations of Nature with a religious significance."

The outer world matters only in so far as it affects the inner. It is the Indian way of experiencing; what is true of Gandhi's autobiography is true of many other Indian autobiographies, though the self-absorption is usually more sterile. "I see people having their being": the Indian girl who said that of the Bombay crowds she saw on her return from Europe was trying hard. She was in the Indian tradition; like Gandhi in Southampton in 1888, she couldn't describe what she hadn't been able to take in. In India, as she said, she "related" only to her family. The vogue word enabled her to boast in a modern-sounding way; but the word also covered up a traditional limitation of vision and response. The deficiency that she was able to convert into boasting is an aspect of what is now being propagated as Hindu wisdom by those holy men who preach "meditation" and expound the idea of the world as illusion.

Meditation and stillness can be a form of therapy. But it may be that the true Hindu bliss—the losing of the self—is more easily accessible to Hindus. According to Dr. Sudhir Kakar, a psychotherapist at Jawaharlal Nehru University in New Delhi, who is himself Indian and has practiced both in Europe and in India, the Indian ego is "underdeveloped," "the world of magic and animistic ways of thinking lie close to the surface," and the Indian grasp of reality "relatively tenuous." "Generally among Indians"—Kakar is working on a book, but this is from a letter—"there seems to be a different relationship to outside reality, compared to one met with in the West. In India it is closer to a certain stage in childhood when outer objects did not have a separate, independent existence but were intimately related to the self and its affective states. They were not something in their own right, but were good or bad, threatening or rewarding, helpful or cruel, all depending on the person's feelings of the moment."

This underdeveloped ego, according to Kakar, is created by the detailed social organization of Indian life, and fits into that life. "The mother functions as the external ego of the child for a much longer period than is customary in the West, and many of the ego functions concerned with reality are later transferred from mother to the family and other social institutions." Caste and clan are more than brotherhoods; they define the individual completely. The individual is never on his own; he is always fundamentally a member of his group, with a complex apparatus of rules, rituals, taboos. Every detail of behavior is regulated—the bowels to be cleared before breakfast and never after, for instance, the left hand and not the right to be used for intimate sexual contact, and so on. Relationships are codified. And religion and religious practices—"magic and animistic ways of thinking"—lock everything into place. The need, then, for individual observation and judgment is reduced; something close to a purely instinctive life becomes possible.

The childlike perception of reality that results does not imply childishness—Gandhi proves the opposite. But it does suggest that Indians are immersed in their experiences in a way that Western people can seldom be. It is less easy for Indians to withdraw and analyze. The difference between the Indian and the Western ways of perceiving comes out most clearly in the sex act. Western man can describe the sex act; even at the moment of orgasm he can observe himself. Kakar says that his Indian patients, men and women, do not have this gift, cannot describe the sex act, are capable only of saying, "It happened."

While his world holds and he is secure, the Indian is a man simply having his being; and he is surrounded by other people having their being. But when the props of family, clan, and caste go, chaos and blankness come. Gandhi in 1888, not yet nineteen, taking ship at Bombay for Southampton, would have been at sea in every way. It was about Gandhi and Gandhi's account of England that I talked to Kakar when we met in Delhi. Gandhi would have had no means of describing what he saw at Southampton on arrival, Kakar said: Gandhi would have been concentrating too fiercely on the turmoil within him; he would have been fighting too hard to hold on to his idea of who he was. (And Kakar is right: later in the autobiography Gandhi says of his first weekend in England, spent at the Victoria Hotel in London: "The stay at that hotel had scarcely been a helpful experience for I had not lived there with my wits about me.")

"We Indians," Kakar says, "use the outside reality to preserve the continuity of the self amidst an ever changing flux of outer events and things." Men do not, therefore, actively explore the world; rather, they are defined by it. It is this negative way of perceiving that goes with "meditation," the striving after the infinite, the bliss of losing the self; it also goes with *karma* and the complex organization of Indian life. Everything locks together; one cannot be isolated from the other. In the Indian set-up, as Kakar says, it is the Western-style "mature personality," individualistic and assertive, that would be the misfit. Which no doubt explains why, in the ashrams, while Indians appear to flourish in the atmosphere of communal holiness, Western inmates, like the hippies elsewhere in India, tend to look sour and somewhat below par.

In an active, busy country, full of passion and controversy, it is not an easy thing to grasp, this negative way of perceiving. Yet it is fundamental to an understanding of India's intellectual second-rateness, which is generally taken for granted but may be the most startling and depressing fact about the world's second most populous country, which now has little to offer the world except its Gandhian concept of holy poverty and the recurring crooked comedy of its holy men, and which, while asserting the antiquity of its civilization (and usually simply asserting, without knowledge or scholarship), is now dependent in every practical way on other, imperfectly understood civilizations.

A recent remarkable novel, however, takes us closer to the Indian idea of the self, and without too much mystification. The novel is *Samskara*, by U. R. Anantamurti, a forty-four-year-old university teacher. Its theme is a brahmin's loss of identity; and it corroborates much of what Sudhir Kakar says. The novel was originally written in Kannada, a language of South India; its India is not over-explained or dressed up or simplified. The novel has now had an India-wide success; it has been made into a prize-winning film; and an English translation (by a poet, A. K. Ramanujan) was serialized over the first three months of 1976 in India's best paper, the *Illustrated Weekly of India*.

The central figure is the Acharya, the spiritual leader of a brotherhood of brahmins. At an early age the Acharya decided that he was a "man of goodness"—that that was his nature, his *karma*, the thing he was programed to be by his previous lives. In the Acharya's reasoning, no one can *become* a man of goodness; he is that, or he isn't; and the "clods," the "men of darkness," cannot complain, because by their nature they have no desire for salvation anyway. It was in obedience to the "good" in his nature that, at the age of sixteen, the Acharya married a crippled girl of twelve. It was his act of sacrifice; the crippled girl was his "sacrificial altar"; and after twenty years the sacrificial act still fills him with pleasure, pride, and compassion. Every day, serving the crippled, ugly woman, even during the pollution of her periods, he gets nearer salvation; and he thinks, "I get ripe and ready." He is famous now, this

Acharya, for his sacrifice, his goodness, and the religious wisdom brought him by his years of study of the palm-leaf scriptures; he is the "crest-jewel of the Vedanta," and the Vedanta is the ultimate wisdom.

But among the brahmin brotherhood there is one who has fallen. He drinks; he catches the sacred fish from the tank of a temple; he mixes with Moslems and keeps an untouchable mistress. He cannot be expelled from the brotherhood. Compassion is one reason, compassion being an aspect of the goodness of the Acharya. But there is another reason: the fallen brahmin threatens to become a Moslem if he is expelled, and such a conversion would retrospectively pollute, and thereby break up, the entire brotherhood. This very wicked brahmin now dies of plague, and a crisis ensues. Should the brotherhood perform the final rites? Only brahmins can perform the rites for another brahmin. But can the dead man be considered a brahmin? In his life he abjured brahminhood, but did brahminhood leave him? Can the brotherhood perform the rites without polluting itself? Can another, lower sect of brahmins be made to perform the rites? (They are willing: the request flatters them: their brahmin line got crossed at some time, and they feel it.) But wouldn't that bring the brotherhood into disrepute—having the rites for one of their own performed by a lower group?

These are the problems that are taken to the Acharya, the crest-jewel, the man of goodness. The matter is urgent. The heat is intense, the body is rotting, the vultures are flapping about, there is a danger of the plague spreading. And the brahmins, who are fussy about their food in every way, are getting hungry: they can't eat while the corpse is uncremated.

But the Acharya cannot give a quick answer. He cannot simply consult his heart, his goodness. The question of the status of the dead man—brahmin or not brahmin, member of the brotherhood or outcaste—is not a moral question. It is a matter of pollution; and it is therefore a matter for the laws, the sacred books. The Acharya has to consult the books; no one knows his way about the palm-leaf manuscripts as well as the Acharya. But this consulting of the books takes time. The plague spreads; some untouchables die and are unceremoniously burned in their huts; the brahmins are beside themselves with hunger and anxiety. And the books give the Acharya no answer.

The Acharya understands that his reputation for wisdom is now at stake; in the midst of the crisis he acknowledges this remnant of personal vanity. But a decision has to be made, and it has to be the correct one. The Acharya can only turn to magic. In the morning he goes to the temple of the monkey god and ritually washes down the man-sized idol. He puts one flower on the god's left shoulder and another on the right. And he decides how the god will answer: if the flower on the right shoulder falls first, the brotherhood can perform the rites for the dead man. But the god gives no reply. For the whole of the hot day, while the Acharya prays and anguishes (and his crippled wife becomes infected by the plague), neither flower falls. And, for the first time in his life, the Acharya, the man of goodness, has doubts about himself: perhaps he is not worthy enough to get an answer from the god.

Exhausted, tormented, he leaves the temple in the evening, to go to look after his wife. In the forest he meets the untouchable mistress of the dead man. She expresses her concern for him; she has worshiped the Acharya for his piety, and it has occurred to her that she should have a child by the Acharya. Her breasts touch him, and he is enveloped by the moment; he wakes at midnight imagining himself a child again, in his mother's lap. It cannot be said that he falls or sins. The words are too positive. As with Sudhir Kakar's patients in real life, the sexual moment simply happens. "It was a sacred moment—nothing before it, nothing after it. A moment that brought into being what never was and then itself went out of being. Formless before, formless after. In between, the embodiment, the moment. Which means I'm absolutely not responsible for making love to her. Not responsible for that moment. But the moment altered me—why?"

The reasoning is strange, but that is now the Acharya's crisis: not guilt, but a sudden neurotic uncertainty about his nature. The earlier crisis has receded: the dead man has been cremated during the night by his mistress, with the help of a Moslem. The Acharya is left with his new anguish. Is he a man of goodness, or has he really all his life belonged to the other, "tigerish" world? Men are what they are, what they have been made by their previous lives. But how does a man know his true nature, his "form"?

"We shape ourselves through our choices, bring form and line to this thing we call our person." But what has been his defining choice—the long life of sacrifice and goodness, or that barely apprehended sexual moment? He doesn't know; he feels only that he has "lost form" and that his person is now like "a demonic premature foetus." He is bound again to the wheel of *karma*; he has to start again from the beginning and make a new decision about his nature. In the meantime he is like a ghost, cut off from the community of men. He has lost God and lost the ways of goodness. "Like a baby monkey losing hold of his grip on the mother's body as she leaps from branch to branch, he felt he had lost hold and fallen from the rites and actions he had clutched till now." Because men are not what they make themselves, there is no question here of faith or conviction or ideals or the perfectability of the self. There is only a wish for knowledge of the self, which alone would make possible a return to the Hindu bliss of the instinctive life: "to be, just to be."

Formless now, his wife dead from the plague, and with her death his especial act of sacrifice abruptly terminated, the Acharya decides to wander, to let his legs take him where they will. This is really an attempt to test his responses to the world; it might be said that he is trying to define his new form by negatives. What do other people see in him? Does the peasant see the brahmin still? Do other brahmins see the brahmin, or do they see a fraud? At a village fair, is he the man to be tempted by the women acrobats, the pollutions of the soda-pop stall and coffee stall, the lower-caste excitement of the cockfight? Between the pollution-free brahmin world and this world, the "world of ordinary pleasures," of darkness, a "demon world of pressing need, revenge and greed," there is no middle way. All around him are "purposive eyes. Eyes engaged in things . . . Immersed. The oneness, the monism, of desire and fulfilment." Men are defined by the world; they are defined by the pollution they can expose themselves to.

The Acharya is terrified; he feels himself being "transformed from ghost to demon." But, neurotically, he continues to test himself. His caste sins mount; and he understands that by exposing himself to pollution he has become a polluting thing himself. He comes to a decision.

He will return to the brotherhood and confess. He will tell them about his sexual adventure with the dead man's untouchable mistress, his visit to the common fair; he will tell them that, though in a state of pollution (partly because of his wife's death), he ate with brahmins in a temple and invited a man of lower caste to eat with him. He will speak without repentance or sorrow. He will simply be telling them about the truth of his inner self, which by a series of accidents—perhaps not really accidents—he has just discovered.

Samskara is a difficult novel, and it may be that not everyone will agree with my reading of it. The translation is not always clear; but many of the Hindu concepts are not easy to render in English. Even so, the narrative is hypnotic; and the brilliance of the writing in the original Kannada can be guessed. Antibrahmin feeling (and by extension anti-Aryan, antinorthern feeling) is strong in the south; and some readers of the serialization in the *Illustrated Weekly of India* have seen the novel as an attack on brahmins. This is a political simplification; but it shows to what extent Indians are able to accept the premises of the novel that are so difficult for an outsider: caste, pollution, the idea of the *karma*-given self, the anguish at the loss of caste identity.

The author, U. R. Anantamurti, is a serious literary man. He teaches English to postgraduate students at Mysore University, which has a lively English department; and he has also taught in the United States. His academic background seems a world away from the society he describes in the novel; and it is hard to assess his attitude to that society. Knowingly or unknowingly, Anantamurti has portrayed a barbaric civilization, where the books, the laws, are

buttressed by magic, and where a too elaborate social
organization is unquickened by intellect or creativity or
ideas of moral responsibility (except to the self in its climb
to salvation). These people are all helpless, disadvantaged,
easily unbalanced; the civilization they have inherited has
long gone sour; living instinctive lives, crippled by rules ("I
didn't try to solve it for myself. I depended on God, on the
old lawbooks. Isn't this precisely why we have created the
Books?"), they make up a society without a head.

References to buses and newspapers and the Congress
Party indicate that the novel is set in modern times. But
the age seems remote; and certainly Gandhi doesn't seem
to have walked this way. The Acharya's anguish about his
true nature, though presented in religious terms, is bound
up with the crudest ideas of pollution and caste and power.
Brahmins must be brahmins, the Acharya reasons at one
stage; otherwise "righteousness" will not prevail. "Won't
the lower castes get out of hand? In this decadent age,
common men follow the right path out of fear—if that
were destroyed, where could we find the strength to uphold
the world?" It is an aspect of this righteousness that when
an untouchable woman begs for a gift of tobacco, the
brahmin woman should throw it out into the street, as to
a dog. In this way pollution is avoided, and righteousness
and fear maintained.

"We Indians use the outer reality to preserve the continuity of the self." Sudhir Kakar's analysis of Gandhi's
stupor in England in 1888 is remarkably like Anantamurti's
wonderful description of the Acharya's wanderings in the
world. Gandhi is preserving his purity, his idea of the self,
in the midst of strangeness. The Acharya is collecting im-
purities; the account he will present to the brotherhood

is not an account of what he has seen, an account of the world he has decided he must enter, but an account of the pollutions he has endured. In both men there is the same limitation of vision and response, the same self-absorption.

But there is an important difference. The Acharya is imprisoned in his dead civilization; he can only define himself within it. He has not, like Gandhi in England, had to work out his faith and decide where—in the wider world— he stands. Gandhi, maturing in alien societies, defensively withdrawing into the self, sinking into his hard-won convictions and vows, becoming more obstinate with age, and always (from his autobiography) seemingly headed for lunacy, is constantly rescued and redefined by external events, the goadings of other civilizations: the terror and strangeness of England, the need to pass the law examinations, the racial pressures of South Africa, British authoritarianism in India (made clear by his experience of the democratic ways of South Africa).

When Gandhi returns to India for good, in his mid-forties, he is fully made; and even at the end, when he is politically isolated and almost all holy man, the pattern of his foreign-created mahatmahood holds. In the turmoil of Independence—the killings, the mass migrations between India and Pakistan, the war in Kashmir—he is still, at the age of seventy-eight, obsessed with the vow of sexual abstinence he had taken forty years before at the time of the Zulu rebellion in South Africa. But he is roused by the Hindu-Muslim massacres in Bengal and goes to the district of Noakhali. Sad last pilgrimage: embittered people scatter broken glass on the roads he is to walk. Seventeen years before, on the Salt March, at the other end of India, the poor had sometimes strewn his path with cool green leaves.

Now, in Bengal, he has nothing to offer except his presence, and he knows it. Yet he is heard to say to himself again and again, "*Kya karun? Kya karun?* What shall I do?" At this terrible moment his thoughts are of action, and he is magnificent.

The Acharya will never know this anguish of frustration. Embracing the "demon world," deliberately living out his newly discovered nature as he deliberately lived out the old, he will continue to be self-absorbed; and his self-absorption will be as sterile as it had been when he was a man of goodness. No idea will come to him, as it came to Gandhi, of the imperfections of the world, of a world that might in some way be put right. The times are decadent, the Acharya thinks (or thought, when he was a man of goodness). But that is only because the lower castes are losing fear and getting out of hand; and the only answer is a greater righteousness, a further withdrawal into the self, a further turning away from the world, a striving after a more instinctive life, where the perception of reality is even weaker and the mind "just one awareness, one wonder."

Restful to the outsider, the visitor, this ideal of diminishing perception. But India has invested in necessary change, and a changing society requires something else. At a time of change, according to Sudhir Kakar, the underdeveloped ego can be a "dangerous luxury." Cities grow; people travel out of their ancestral districts; the ties of clan and family are loosened. The need for sharper perception increases; and perception has to become "an individual rather than a social function."

This threatens everything; it unbalances people in a way outsiders can hardly understand. Caste and clan and security and faith and shallow perception all go together; one cannot be altered or developed without damaging the rest. How can anyone used from infancy to the security of the group, and the security of a minutely regulated life, become an individual, a man on his own? He will be drowned in the immensity of the unknown world; he will be lost. He will be like the Acharya in Anantamurti's novel, tormented by his formlessness. "A piece of string in the wind, a cloud taking on shapes according to the wind. I've become a thing. By an act of will, I'll become human again."

For the Acharya there is a sanctioned way to becoming human again; he has only to make a choice. But how does a man become an individual when there is no path, and no knowledge even of the goal? How can men learn to presume? Men can only stumble through events, holding on to the idea of the self. When caste and family simplify relationships, and the sanctity of the laws cannot be doubted, when magic buttresses the laws, and the epics and legends satisfy the imagination, and astrologers know the future anyway, men cannot easily begin to observe and analyze. And how, it might be asked, can Indians face the Indian reality without some filter of faith or magic? How often in India—at every level—rational conversation about the country's problems trails away into talk of magic, of the successful prophecies of astrologers, of the wisdom of auspicious hours, of telepathic communications, and actions taken in response to some inner voice! It is always there, this knowledge of the other, regulated world, undermining, or balancing, intellect and the beginnings of painful perception.

When men cannot observe, they don't have ideas; they have obsessions. When people live instinctive lives, something like a collective amnesia steadily blurs the past. Few educated Indians now remember or acknowledge their serenity in 1962, before the Chinese war and the end of the Nehru era, when Independence could still be enjoyed as personal dignity alone, and it could be assumed, from the new possession of dignity by so many, that India had made it or was making it. Few can interpret the increasing frenzy of the country since then, through the Pakistan war of 1965, the consequent financial distress, the drought and famine of 1967, the long agony of the Bangladesh crisis of 1971.

India is poor: the fact has only recently begun to be observed in India, with the great growth in population, the choking of the cities, the political assertiveness of industrial workers. To many Indians, however, poverty, just discovered, also seems to have just been created. It is, bizarrely, one of the charges most often made against Mrs. Gandhi: her failure to remove poverty, as she promised in 1971: that very poverty which, until the other day, was regarded by everyone else as a fact of Indian life, and holy, a cause for pious Gandhian pride.

A famous Indian politician, in his time a man of great power, once almost prime minister, said to a foreign interviewer just before the Emergency: "Here there's no rice, there's no wheat. . . . Until five years ago a family used to buy at least twenty pounds of cereals a month. . . . We built factories too . . . and machinery we even managed to export. . . . Now we have to import everything once more." Did he really believe what he said? No rice, no wheat, everything imported? Did he really believe in that picture of a recent richer past? The chances are that he did. He is a Gandhian, and will not consciously distort the truth. He sits at his spinning wheel every day: the Gandhian spinning wheel no longer a means of livelihood for the dispossessed, or a symbol of labor and brotherhood with the poor, but a sacred tool, an aid to thought (as with this politician) or (as with others) a yogic means of stilling the waves of the mind, an aid to mental vacuity. To know the past (when he had been a man of power) the old politician had only to consult himself, his heart. There he saw quite clearly his own fulfillment and—since the outer world matters only in so far as it affects the inner—he could claim without disingenuousness that there had been a time when things were going well with the country.

Individual obsessions coalesce into political movements; and in the last ten years or so these movements of protest have become wilder. Many of these movements look back to the past, which they reinterpret to suit their needs. Some, like the Shiv Sena in Bombay (looking back two and a half centuries to the period of Maratha glory) and the Dravidian movement in the south (seeking to revenge itself, after three thousand years, on the Aryan north), have positive regenerating effects. Others, like the Anand Marg, fusing disparate obsessions, asserting caste and violence and sexual laxity as if in an inversion of Gandhianism, are the grossest kind of Hindu cult: a demonstration, like others in the past, of the ease with which Hinduism, striving after internal continuity and calm, stripping itself of intellect and the need for intellect, can decline into barbarism.

A party which seeks a nuclear armory for India, and combines that with a program for protecting the holy cow (free fodder for cows, homes for old cows), might at first be dismissed as a joke. But it isn't a joke. This party is the Jan Sangh, the National Party. It is the best-organized opposition party; with its emphasis on Hindu power, it touches many Hindu hearts, and it has a large middle-class following in the cities; for some years it controlled the Delhi municipality. In the 1971 elections one of its candidates in Delhi ran purely on the cow issue.

It might all seem only part of the quaintness of India. It is in fact an aspect of the deep disturbance of India at a time of difficult change, when many men, like the Acharya in Anantamurti's novel, find themselves thrown out into the world and formless, and strive, in the only ways open to them, to become human again.

2

With the Emergency some of these parties have been banned and their leaders imprisoned, with many others; and people outside who are concerned about the rule of law in India have sometimes been disconcerted by the causes they have found themselves sponsoring. In India, where the problems are beyond comprehension, the goals have to be vague. The removal of poverty, the establishment of justice: these, however often stated now, are like abstractions. People's obsessions are more immediate.

One opposition pamphlet now being circulated is about the torture of political prisoners in Indian jails. The torture, it must be said, is not of the systematized South American variety; it is more an affair of random brutality. But the power of the police in India is now unlimited, and the pamphlet doesn't exaggerate. It leaves out only the fact that there has always been torture of this sort in Indian jails. Torture, like poverty, is something about India that Indians have just discovered.

There is something else about the pamphlet. It lists a number of strange things as tortures. Somebody's mustache was shaved off; many people were beaten with shoes and made to walk the public streets with shoes on their heads; some people had their faces blackened and were paraded in the bazaar in cycle-rickshaws; one university professor "was pushed from side to side with smearing remarks." These are not what are usually thought of as tortures; they are caste pollutions, more permanently wounding, and a greater cause for hysteria, than any beating-up. Black is a color horrible to the Indo-Aryan; the mustache is an important caste emblem, and untouchables can be killed for wearing their mustaches curling up rather than drooping down; shoes are made of leather and tread the polluted earth. Almost without knowing it, the pamphlet confuses its causes: democracy, the rule of law, and humanitarianism merge in caste outrage. Men are so easily thrown back into the self, so easily lose the wider view. In this land of violence and cruelty, in the middle of a crisis that threatens the intellectual advance India has begun to make, the underdeveloped ego is still capable of an alarming innocence.

6

Synthesis and Mimicry

1

At a dinner party in Delhi, a young foreign academic, describing what was most noticeable about the crowds he had seen in Bombay on his Indian holiday, said with a giggle: "They were doing their 'potties' on the street." He was adding to what his Indian wife had said with mystical gravity: she saw people only having their being. She was middle-class and well connected. He was shallow and brisk and common, enjoying his pickings, swinging happily from branch to low branch in the grove of Academe. But the couple were well matched in an important way. Her Indian blindness to India, with its roots in caste and religion, was like his foreigner's easy disregard. The combination is not new; it has occurred again and again in the last thousand years of Indian history, the understanding based on Indian misunderstanding; and India has always been the victim.

But this couple lived outside India. They returned from time to time as visitors, and India restored in different ways the self-esteem of each. For other people in that gathering, however, who lived in India and felt the new threat of the millions and all the uncertainties that had come with Independence and growth, India could no longer be taken for granted. The poor had ceased to be background. Another way of looking was felt to be needed, some profounder acknowledgment of the people of the streets.

And this was what was attempted by another young woman, a friend of the couple who lived abroad. The women of Bombay, she said, and she meant the women of the lower castes, wore a certain kind of sari and preferred certain colors; the men wore a special kind of turban. She had lived in Bombay; but, already, she was wrong: it is true that the women dress traditionally, but in Bombay the men for the most part wear trousers and shirt. It was a revealing error: for all her sympathy with the poor, she was still receptive only to caste signals, and was as blind as her friend.

"I will tell you about the poor people in Bombay," she insisted. "They are beautiful. They are more beautiful than the people in this room." But now she was beginning to lie. She spoke with passion, but she didn't believe what she said. The poor of Bombay are not beautiful, even with their picturesque costumes in low-caste colors. In complexion, features, and physique the poor are distinct from the well-to-do; they are like a race apart, a dwarf race, stunted and slow-witted and made ugly by generations of undernourishment; it will take generations to rehabilitate them. The idea that the poor are beautiful was, with this girl, a borrowed idea. She had converted it into a political attitude, which she was prepared to defend. But it had not sharpened her perception.

New postures in India, attitudes that imply new ways of seeing, often turn out to be a matter of words alone. In their attempts to go beyond the old sentimental abstractions about the poverty of India, and to come to terms with the poor, Indians have to reach outside their civilization, and they are at the mercy then of every kind of imported idea. The intellectual confusion is greater now than in the days of the British, when the world seemed to stand still, the issues were simpler, and it was enough for India to assert its Indianness. The poor were background then. Now they press hard, and have to be taken into account.

From the *Indian Express*, October 31, 1975:

> Education Minister Prabha Rau has urged scientists and technologists to innovate simpler technology so that it does not become exclusive. Mrs. Rau was speaking as the chief guest at a seminar on science and integrated rural development. . . . She lamented the fact that the youth were not interested in science and technology because "it is not only expensive but the exclusive preserve of a few," and hoped that there would be more "active participation of a larger number of people."

The speech is not easy to understand—the reporter was clearly baffled by what he heard—but it seems to contain a number of different ideas. There is the idea that the poor should also be educated (Indian students, who are assumed in the speech to be middle-class, *are* in fact interested in science); there is the idea that development should affect the greatest number; and there is the new, and unrelated, idea about "intermediate technology," the idea that Indian technology should match Indian resources and take into account the nature of Indian society. The first two ideas are unexceptionable, the third more complex; but, complex or simple, the ideas are so much a matter of words that they have been garbled together—either by the minister or by the reporter—into a kind of political manifesto, an expression of concern with the poor.

The poor are almost fashionable. And this idea of intermediate technology has become an aspect of that fashion. The cult in India centers on the bullock cart. The bullock cart is not to be eliminated; after three thousand or more backward years Indian intermediate technology will now improve the bullock cart. "Do you know," someone said to me in Delhi, "that the investment in bullock carts is equivalent to the total investment in the railways?" I had always had my doubts about bullock carts; but I didn't know until then that they were not cheap, were really quite expensive (more expensive than many second-hand cars in England), and that only richer peasants could afford them. It seemed to me a great waste, the kind of waste that poverty perpetuates. But I was glad I didn't speak, because the man who was giving me these statistics went on: "Now. If we could improve the performance of the bullock cart by ten percent..."

What did it mean, improving the performance by ten percent? Greater speed, bigger loads? Were there bigger loads to carry? These were not the questions to ask, though. Intermediate technology had decided that the bullock cart was to be improved. Metal axles, bearings, rubber tires? But wouldn't that make the carts even more expensive? Wouldn't it take generations, and a lot of money, to introduce those improvements? And, having got so far, mightn't it be better to go just a little further and introduce some harmless little engine? Shouldn't intermediate technology be concentrating on that harmless little engine capable of the short journeys bullock carts usually make?

But no: these were a layman's fantasies: the bullock was, as it were, central to the bullock-cart problem, as the problem had been defined. The difficulty—for science—was the animal's inconvenient shape. The bullock wasn't like the horse; it couldn't be harnessed properly. The bullock carried a yoke on its neck. This had been the practice since the beginning of history, and the time had come for change. This method of yoking was not only inefficient; it also created sores and skin cancer on the bullock's neck and shortened the animal's working life. The bullock-cart enthusiast in Delhi told me that a bullock lasted only three years. But this was the exaggeration of enthusiasm; other people told me that bullocks lasted ten or eleven years. To improve yoking, much research had to be done on the stresses on the bullock as it lifted and pulled. The most modern techniques of monitoring had to be used; and somewhere in the south there was a bullock which, while apparently only going about its peaceful petty business, was as wired up as any cosmonaut.

I was hoping to have a look at this animal when I got to the south and—India being a land of overenthusiastic report—to check with the scientist who had become the bullock-cart king. But the man himself was out of the country, lecturing; he was in demand abroad. Certain subjects, like poverty and intermediate technology, keep the experts busy. They are harassed by international seminars and conferences and foundation fellowships. The rich countries pay; they dictate the guiding ideas, which are the ideas of the rich about the poor, ideas sometimes about what is good for the poor, and sometimes no more than expressions of alarm. They, the rich countries, even manage now to export their romantic doubts about industrial civilization. These are the doubts that attend every kind of great success; and they are romantic because they contain no wish to undo that success or to lose the fruits of that success. But India interprets these doubts in its own debilitating way, and uses them to reconcile itself to its own failure.

Complex imported ideas, forced through the retort of Indian sensibility, often come out cleansed of content, and harmless; they seem so regularly to lead back, through religion and now science, to the past and nullity: to the spinning wheel, the bullock cart. Intermediate technology should mean a leap ahead, a leap beyond accepted solutions, new ways of perceiving coincident needs and resources. In India it has circled back to something very like the old sentimentality about poverty and the old ways, and has stalled with the bullock cart: a fascinating intellectual adventure for the people concerned, but sterile, divorced from reality and usefulness.

And while, in the south, science seeks to improve the bullock cart, at Ahmedabad in Gujarat, at the new, modern, and expensively equipped National Institute of Design, they are—on a similar "intermediate" principle and as part of the same cult of the poor—designing or redesigning tools for the peasants. Among the finished products in the glass-walled showroom downstairs was a portable agricultural spraying machine, meant to be carried on the back. The bright yellow plastic casing looked modern enough; but it was hard to know why at Ahmedabad—apart from the anxiety to get the drab thing into bright modern plastic—they had felt the need to redesign this piece of equipment, which on the tea gardens and elsewhere is commonplace and, it might be thought, sufficiently reduced to simplicity. Had something been added? Something had, within the yellow plastic. A heavy motor, which would have crippled the peasant called upon to carry it for any length of time: the peasant who already, in some parts of India, has to judge tools by their weight and, because he has sometimes to carry his plough long distances to his field, prefers a wooden plough to an iron one. My guide acknowledged that the spray was heavy, but gave no further explanation.

The spraying machine, however, was of the modern age. Upstairs, a fourth-year student, clearly one of the stars of the Institute, was designing tools for the ancient world. He had a knife-sharpening machine to show; but in what way it differed from other cumbersome knife-sharpening machines I couldn't tell. His chief interest, though, was in tools for reaping. He disapproved of the sickle for some reason; and he was against the scythe because the cut stalks fell too heavily to the ground. Scythe and sickle were to be replaced by a long-handled tool which looked like a pair of edging shears: roughly made, no doubt because it was for the peasants and had to be kept rough and simple. When placed on the ground, the thick metal blades made a small V; but only one blade was movable, and this blade the peasant had to kick against the fixed blade and then—by means the designer had not yet worked out—retract for the next cut.

As an invention, this seemed to me some centuries behind the reaping machine of ancient Rome (a bullock-pushed tray with a serrated edge); but the designer, who was a townsman, said he had spent a week in the countryside and the peasants had been interested. I said that the tool required the user to stand; Indians preferred to squat while they did certain jobs. He said the people had to be reeducated.

His alternative design absolutely required standing. This was a pair of reaping shoes. At the front of the left shoe was a narrow cutting blade; on the right side of the right shoe was a longer curved blade. So the peasant, advancing through his ripe corn, would kick with his left foot and cut, while with his right he would describe a wide arc and cut: a harvest dance. Which, I felt, explained the otherwise mysterious presence of a wheelchair in the showroom downstairs, among the design items—the yellow agricultural spray, the boards with the logos for various firms, the teacups unsteady on too stylishly narrow a base. The wheelchair must have been for peasants: the hand-propelled inner wheel of the chair, if my trial was valid, would bark the invalid's knuckles against the outer wheel, and the chair itself, when stopped, would tip the invalid forward. Yes, my guide said neutrally, the chair did do that: the invalid had to remember to sit well back.

Yet the chair was in the window as something to show, something designed; and perhaps it was there for no better reason than that it looked modern and imported, proof that India was going ahead. Going ahead downstairs, going piously backward upstairs: India advancing simultaneously on all fronts, responding to every kind of idea at once. The National Institute of Design is the only one of its kind in India; it is fabulously equipped, competition to enter is fierce, and standards should be high. But it is an imported idea, an imported institution, and it has been imported whole, just like that. In India it has been easily divorced from its animating principle, reduced to its equipment, and has ended—admittedly after a controversial period: a new administrator had just been sent in—as a finishing school for the unacademic young, a play-pen, with artisans called in to do the heavy work, like those dispirited men I saw upstairs squatting on the floor and working on somebody's chairs: India's eternal division of labor, frustrating the proclaimed social purpose of the Institute.

Mimicry within mimicry, imperfectly understood idea within imperfectly understood idea: the second-year girl student in the printing department, not understanding the typographical exercise she had been set, and playing with type like a child with a typewriter, avoiding, in the name of design, anything like symmetry, clarity, or logic; the third-year girl student showing a talentless drawing and saying, in unacknowledged paraphrase of Klee, that she had described "the adventures of a line"; and that fourth-year man playing with tools for the peasants. There are times when the intellectual confusion of India seems complete and it seems impossible to get back to clarifying first principles. Which must have been one of the aims of an institute of design: to make people look afresh at the everyday.

An elementary knowledge of the history of technology would have kept that student—and the teachers who no doubt encouraged him—off the absurdity of his tools; even an elementary knowledge of the Indian countryside, elementary vision. Those tools were designed in an institute where there appeared to have been no idea of the anguish of the Indian countryside: the landless or bonded laborers, the child laborers, the too many cheap hands, the petty chopped-up fields, the nullity of the tasks. The whole project answered a fantasy of the peasant's life: the peasant as the man overburdened by the unending labors of his fields, overburdened by the need to gather in his abundant harvest: romance, an idea of the simplicity of the past and preindustrial life, which is at the back of so much thinking, political and otherwise, in India, the vision based on no vision.

The bullock cart is to be improved by high science. The caravans will plod idyllically to market, and the peasant, curled up on his honest load, will sleep away the night, a man matching his rhythm to that of nature, a man in partnership with his animals. But that same peasant, awake, will goad his bullock in the immemorial way, by pushing a stick up its anus. It is an unregarded but necessary part of the idyll, one of the obscene sights of the Indian road: the hideous cruelty of preindustrial life, cruelty constant and casual, and easily extended from beast to man.

The beauty of the simple life, the beauty of the poor: in India the ideas are rolled together and appear one, but the ideas are separate and irreconcilable, because they assert two opposed civilizations.

2

Indians say that their gift is for cultural synthesis. When they say this, they are referring to the pre-British past, to the time of Moslem dominance. And though the idea is too much part of received wisdom, too much a substitute for thought and inquiry, there is proof of that capacity for synthesis in Indian painting. For the two hundred years or so of its vigor, until (very roughly) about 1800, this art is open to every kind of influence, even European. It constantly alters and develops as it shifts from center to center and is full of local surprises. Its inventiveness—which contemporary scholarship is still uncovering—is truly astonishing.

In the nineteenth century, with the coming of the British, this great tradition died. Painting is only as good as its patrons allow it to be. Indian painting, before the British, was an art of the princely courts, Hindu or Moslem, and reflected the culture of those courts. Now there were new patrons, of more limited interests; and nothing is sadder, in the recent history of Indian culture, than to see Indian painting, in its various schools, declining into East India Company art, tourist art. A new way of looking is imposed, and Indian artists become ordinary as they depict native "types" in as European a manner as their techniques allow, or when, suppressing their own idea of their function as craftsmen, their own feeling for design and organization, they struggle with what must have been for them the meaninglessness of Constable-like "views." A vigorous art becomes imitative, second-rate, insecure (always with certain regional exceptions); it knows it cannot compete; it withers away, and is finally abolished by the camera. It is as though, in a conquered Europe, with all of European art abruptly disregarded, artists were required to paint genre pictures in, say, a Japanese manner. It can be done, but the strain will kill.

India has recovered its traditions of the classical dance, once almost extinct, and its weaving arts. But the painting tradition remains broken; painting cannot simply go back to where it left off; too much has intervened. The Indian past can no longer provide inspiration for the Indian present. In this matter of artistic vision the West is too dominant, and too varied; and India continues imitative and insecure, as a glance at the advertisements and illustrations of any Indian magazine will show. India, without its own living traditions, has lost the ability to incorporate and adapt; what it borrows it seeks to swallow whole. For all its appearance of cultural continuity, for all the liveliness of its arts of dance, music, and cinema, India is incomplete: a whole creative side has died. It is the price India has had to pay for its British period. The loss balances the intellectual recruitment during this period, the political self-awareness (unprecedented in Indian history), and the political reorganization.

What is true of Indian painting is also true of Indian architecture. There again a tradition has been broken; too much has intervened; and modernity, or what is considered to be modernity, has now to be swallowed whole. The effect is calamitous. Year by year India's stock of barely usable modern buildings grows. Old ideas about ventilation are out; modern air-conditioners are in; they absolve the architect of the need to design for the difficult climate, and leave him free to copy. Ahmedabad doesn't only have the National Institute of Design; it also, as a go-ahead city, has a modern little airport building. The roof isn't flat or sloping, but wavy; and the roof is low. Hot air can't rise too high; and glass walls, decoratively hung with some reticulated modern fabric, let in the Indian afternoon sun. It is better to stay with the taxi-drivers outside, where the temperature is only about a hundred. Inside, fire is being fought with fire, modernity with modernity; the glass oven hums with an expensive, power-consuming "Gulmarg" air-cooler, around which the respectable and sheltered cluster.

At Jaisalmer in the Rajasthan desert the state government has just built a tourist guest house of which it is very proud. Little rooms open off a central corridor, and the desert begins just outside the uncanopied windows. But the rooms needn't be stuffy. For ten rupees extra a day you can close the shutters, switch on the electric light, and use the cooler, an enormous factory fan set in the window, which makes the little room roar. Yet Jaisalmer is famous for its old architecture, its palaces, and the almost Venetian grandeur of some of its streets. And in the bazaar area there are traditional courtyard houses, in magnificent stone versions for the desert: tall, permitting ventilation in the outer rooms, some part of the house always in cool shadow.

But the past is the past; architecture in India is a modern course of study and, as such, another imported skill, part of someone else's tradition. In architecture as in art, without the security of a living tradition, India is disadvantaged. Modernity—or Indianness—is so often only a matter of a façade; within, and increasingly, even in remote places now, it is a nightmare of misapplied technology or misunderstood modern design: the rooms built as if for Siberia, always artificially lit, noisy with the power-consuming air-conditioning unit, and uninhabitable without that unit, which leaks down the walls and ruins the fitted carpet: expense upon expense, the waste with which ignorance often burdens poverty.

There was a time when Indians who had been abroad and picked up some simple degree or skill said that they had become displaced and were neither of the East nor West. In this they were absurd and self-dramatizing: they carried India with them, Indian ways of perceiving. Now, with the great migrant rush, little is heard of that displacement. Instead, Indians say that they have become too educated for India. The opposite is usually true: they are not educated enough; they only want to repeat their lessons. The imported skills are rooted in nothing; they are skills separate from principles.

On the train going back to Bombay one rainy evening I heard the complaint from a blank-faced, plump young man. He was too educated for India, he said; and he spoke the worn words without irony or embarrassment. He had done a course in computers in the United States, and (having money) what he wanted to do was to set up a factory to build the American equipment he had learned about. But India wasn't ready for this kind of advanced equipment, and he was thinking he might have to go back permanently to the United States.

I wanted to hear more about his time in the United States. But he had little else to say about that country or— the rainy, smoky industrial outskirts of Bombay, rust, black, and green, going past our window—about India. America was as he had expected it to be, he said. He gave no concrete details. And India—even after the United States, and in spite of what could be seen through our window—he assessed only as an entrepreneur might assess it.

He was of a northern merchant caste; he carried caste in his manner. He belonged to old India; nothing had happened to shake him out of that security; he questioned nothing. From the outside world he had snatched no more than a skill in computers, as in less complicated times he might have learned about cloth or grain at home. He said he was too educated for India. But—to give the example given me by the engineer I had got to know in Bombay— he was like the plumber from the slums: a man from a simple background called upon to exercise a high skill, and exercising it blindly. Water is the plumber's business; but water is to him a luxury, something for which his wife has to stand in line every morning; he cannot then understand why it is necessary for a tap to be placed straight, in the center of a tile. So—in spite of his own simple background, in spite of India—the computer man, possessing only his specialized skill, saw his business as the laying down of computers, anywhere.

To match technology to the needs of a poor country calls for the highest skills, the clearest vision. Old India, with all its encouragements to the instinctive, nonintellectual life, limits vision. And the necessary attempt at making imported technology less "exclusive"—to use the confusing and perhaps confused word of the Maharashtra education minister—has ended with the school of the bullock cart, a mixture of mimicry and fantasy. Yet it is something—perhaps a great deal—that India has felt the need to make the attempt.

3

India is old, and India continues. But all the disciplines and skills that India now seeks to exercise are borrowed. Even the ideas Indians have of the achievements of their civilization are essentially the ideas given them by European scholars in the nineteenth century. India by itself could not have rediscovered or assessed its past. Its past was too much with it, was still being lived out in the rituals, the laws, the magic—the complex instinctive life that muffles response and buries even the idea of inquiry. Indian painting now has its scholars in India, but the approach to painting, even among educated people, is still, generally iconographic, the recognition of deities and themes. A recently dead tradition, an unchanging belief: the creative loss passes unnoticed.

India blindly swallows its past. To understand that past, it has had to borrow alien academic disciplines; and, as with the technology, their foreign origin shows. Much historical research has been done; but European methods of historical inquiry, arising out of one kind of civilization, with its own developing ideas of the human condition, cannot be applied to Indian civilization; they miss too much. Political or dynastic events, economic life, cultural trends: the European approach elucidates little, has the effect of an unsuccessful attempt to equate India with Europe, and makes nonsense of the stops and starts of Indian civilization, the brief flowerings, the long periods of sterility, men forever claimed by the instinctive life, continuity turning to barbarism.

History, with its nationalist shrillness, sociology with its mathematical approach and its tables: these borrowed disciplines remain borrowed. They have as yet given India little idea of itself. India no more possesses Indian history than it possesses its art. People have an idea of the past and can quote approving things from foreign sources (a habit of which all Indians complain and of which all are guilty). But to know India, most people look inward. They consult themselves: in their own past, in the nature of their caste or clan life, their family traditions, they find the idea of India which they know to be true, and according to which they act.

Indian newspapers reflect this limited vision, this absence of inquiry, the absence of what can be called human interest. The precensorship liveliness of the Indian press—of which foreign observers have spoken—was confined to the editorial pages. Elsewhere there were mainly communiqués, handouts, reports of speeches and functions. Indian journalism developed no reporting tradition; it often reported on India as on a foreign country. An unheadlined item from the *Statesman*, September 17, 1975:

> *Woman Jumps to Death:* A woman jumped to death after throwing her two children into a well at Chennaptna, 60 km from Bangalore recently, according to police—PTI.

Recently! But that is all; the police communiqué is enough; no reporter was sent out to get the story. From the *Times of India*, October 4, 1975:

> An "eye-surgeon," who had performed 70 eye operations here in February resulting in the loss of eyesight of 20 persons and serious injuries to many others, has been arrested in Muzaffarnagar, the police said there yesterday. The man, apparently an Ayurvedic physician with no knowledge of surgery, had promised patients in Jalgaon that he would perform the operations at concessional rates.

That is all; the story is over; there will be no more tomorrow.

A caste vision: what is remote from me is remote from me. The Indian press has interpreted its function in an Indian way. It has not sought to put India in touch with itself; it doesn't really know how, and it hasn't felt the need. During its free years it watched over nothing; away from the political inferno of its editorial pages it saw few causes for concern. Its India was background, was going on. It was a small-circulation left-wing paper, the *Economic and Political Weekly* of Bombay, that exposed the abuses on the coalfields in the Dhanbad district of Bihar, where workers were terrorized by moneylenders and their gangs. Shortly after the Emergency, the government announced that two or three hundred of the moneylenders had been arrested. That, too, was a simple agency item in the Indian daily press. No paper related it to what had gone before, or seemed to understand its importance; no one went out to investigate the government's claim. Only, some time later, the Calcutta *Statesman* carried an account by a reporter of what it felt like to go down a pit at Dhanbad: a "color" piece, cast in terms of personal adventure, an Indian account, with the miners as background.

Since the Emergency the government—for obvious reasons—has decreed that newspapers should look away from politics and concentrate on social issues. It has required newspapers to go in for "investigative reporting"— the borrowed words are used; and it might be said that the news about India in the Indian press has never been so bad as it is now. Recent numbers of the *Illustrated Weekly of India* (adventurously edited, even before the Emergency) have carried features on bonded labor, child labor, and child marriage. The Indian press has at last begun to present India to itself. But it does so under compulsion. It is one of the paradoxes of India under the Emergency that make judgment about the Emergency so difficult: the dangers are obvious, but the results can appear positive. The press has lost its political freedom, but it has extended its interpretive function.

The press (like technology, eventually) can be made to match Indian needs. But what of the law? How can that system, bequeathed to India by another civilization with other values, give India equity and perform the law's constant reassessing, reforming role? From the *Times of India*, October 5, 1975:

The Prime Minister, Mrs. Indira Gandhi, said today that the Indian legal system should assume a "dynamic role" in the process of social transformation, shaking off the "inhibiting legacy of the colonial past." . . . She said: "Law should be an instrument of social justice." Explaining the "dynamic role" of the legal system, Mrs. Gandhi said it should assist in the liberation of the human spirit and of human institutions from the strait-jacket of outdated customs. She said the people's respect for law depended on the extent of their conviction that it afforded them real and impartial protection. "Our ancients realized this when they stated that society should uphold dharma so that dharma sustains society," she added.

But how can the imported system assume its dynamic role in India? The difficulty, the contradiction, lies in that very concept of *dharma*. The *dharma* of which Mrs. Gandhi speaks is a complex word: it can mean the faith, pietas, everything which is felt to be right and religious and sanctioned. Law must serve *dharma* or at least not run counter to it; and that seems fair enough. Yet *dharma*, as expressed in the Indian social system, is so shot through with injustice and cruelty, based on such a limited view of man. It can accommodate bonded labor as, once, it accommodated widow-burning. *Dharma* can resist the idea of equity. Law in India can at times appear a forensic game, avoiding collision with the abuses it should be remedying; and it is hard to see how any system of law can do otherwise while the Indian social system holds, and while *dharma* is honored above the simple rights of men.

A. S. R. Chari is a famous Indian criminal lawyer. He has written a book about some of his cases; and in October 1975 *Blitz*, a popular left-wing weekly of Bombay, retold this story from the Chari book. In Maharashtra, in the

1950s, a marriage was arranged between the daughter of a cloth-seller and the son of a lawyer. The lawyer turned up for the wedding ceremony with 150 guests, all to be fed and lodged at the cloth-seller's expense. The cloth-seller objected; the lawyer, angered by the discourtesy and apparent meanness, threw two thousand rupees in notes at the feet of the cloth-seller in a gesture of insult. Yet the marriage went ahead: the lawyer's son married the cloth-seller's daughter. Only, the lawyer forbade his son to have anything more to do with his wife's family, and forbade his daughter-in-law to visit her parents. The girl suffered. ("She seemed to have been a highly strung girl," Chari writes.) She suffered especially when she was not allowed to visit her sister in hospital. Her husband was firm when she asked his permission. He said: "You know the position. I cannot allow this. Do not be too unhappy over it." Waking up that night, the young man found his wife dead beside him.

Cyanide was detected in the viscera of the dead girl; and the young man was charged with her murder. The prosecution argued that she could not, by herself, have obtained the cyanide in Bombay; it must have been administered by her husband, who, as a photographer, had chemicals of various kinds in his laboratory. But the police hadn't found potassium or sodium cyanide in the laboratory; they had only found potassium ferricyanide, not a poison. This gave Chari—arguing the young's man's appeal against conviction for murder—his clue. "Potassium ferricyanide, though not ordinarily a poison, would act as a poison when taken by a person who had hyper-acidity—that is, a person who secreted too much hydrochloric acid in the stomach." So the girl had committed suicide. Her husband was acquitted.

Justice was done. But the injustice to the dead girl was

hardly commented on. The Supreme Court, hearing the appeal, spoke of "false ideas of family prestige"; but in Chari's legalistic account, as rendered in *Blitz*, full of technicalities about the admissibility of evidence, the punishment of the cloth-seller by the suicide of his daughter is made to appear just one of those things. "Oh yes," one of the appeal judges said, "you have to make arrangements so thoroughly that you satisfy every demand made by any one of the bridegroom's party." And in this acknowledgment of the traditional demands of family honor the tragedy of the girl is lost: writing letters to the family she is not allowed to see ("God's will be done"), so quickly accepting that her young life is spoiled and has to be ended.

The law avoids the collision with *dharma*. Yet it is this *dharma* that the law must grapple with if the law is to have a "dynamic role." That is the difficulty: to cope with the new pressures, India has in some ways to undermine itself, to lose its old security. Borrowed institutions can no longer function simply as borrowed institutions, a tribute to modernity. Indians say that their gift is for synthesis. It might be said, rather, that for too long, as a conquered people, they have been intellectually parasitic on other civilizations. To survive in subjection, they have preserved their sanctuary of the instinctive, uncreative life, converting that into a religious ideal; at a more worldly level, they have depended on others for the ideas and institutions that make a country work. The Emergency—coming so soon after Independence—dramatizes India's creative incapacity, its intellectual depletion, its defenselessness, the inadequacy of every Indian's idea of India.

7

Paradise Lost

1

"We are like a zoo," the melancholy middle-class lady said
in Delhi. "Perhaps we should charge."

She lived in India: I was a visitor. She intended a rebuke,
possibly an insult, but it was easy to let it pass. India was
like a zoo because India was poor and cruel and had lost its
way. These were things about India that, with the Emergency, she had just discovered; and they were more than
intellectual discoveries. Once—like other middle-class people, like other people secure in their caste world—she might
have been able to detach herself from the mess of India;
now she felt she was going down with it.

Her husband was connected with the opposition; his
career was suddenly jeopardized; he lived in fear of arrest.
In the pre-Emergency days—when the students were riot-
ing, the unions were striking, and it seemed possible to get
rid of Mrs. Gandhi's government and give India a fresh

start—he had been a figure. Now all his political boldness had turned to hysteria. Action had ceased to be possible; the revolution at whose head he thought he was marching had vanished, leaving him exposed.

"Thousands of us will surround her house to prevent her going out or receiving visitors. We'll camp there night and day, shouting to her to resign. Even if the police arrest us, beat us up, slaughter us. How many can they slaughter? And what will they do with the corpses?" This was what old Mr. Desai, a famous Gandhian and once deputy prime minister, had promised a foreign interviewer. But then, just a few hours later, Mr. Desai had been arrested, no doubt to his own surprise ("I prefer to believe that before committing such a monstrosity Mrs. Gandhi would commit suicide," he had told the interviewer, unwittingly showing up the vanity and shoddiness of his Gandhian posture). And there had been no uprising, no corpses in front of Mrs. Gandhi's house in New Delhi.

Jaya Prakash Narayan, the most respected opposition leader, had been wiser. In his last public speech, in New Delhi, the evening before his arrest, he asked the students in his audience: "Will you go to classes or to prison?" "Prison!" they had replied. And he had said, "Let us see." And the students, when the time came, had done nothing; they had become part of the great peace of the Emergency.

The revolution had turned out to be no revolution. And India, which only a few weeks before had seemed capable of renewed Gandhian fervor, had become like a zoo. The sad lady sat forward on her chair, knees apart below the wrappings of her sari, and looked down at the floor, shaking her head slowly from side to side, as though contemplating the depth of the Indian tragedy; while her husband, speaking above the traffic noise that came through the open windows, offered visions of the repression to come.

He extended his personal anxieties to the country: he foresaw that the British-built "garden city" of New Delhi, now inherited by the Indian rulers of India, would soon be barricaded against the poor and guarded by machine guns. I thought he was exaggerating, but he said that the expulsion of the poor had already begun. A squatters' settlement in the Diplomatic Enclave had been leveled, and people and their possessions thrown out in the rain.

Many weeks later this municipal event was to appear in a London newspaper as hot news from the new India: the overthrow of socialism, the beginning of the assault on the poor: Indian events given a South American interpretation, and thereby made easier for everyone. The report was to catch the very hysteria with which the news had been given to me. But I remembered, that evening in Delhi, that such expulsions of illegal squatters were not new. In 1962, at the time of my first visit to the Indian capital, while Mr. Nehru still ruled, a similar kind of settlement had been bulldozed in the middle-class Defense Colony area. For days the collapsed brown-black spread of thatch and sacking and mud had remained beside the highway—it was as though the people who had lived there had been snuffed out, blown away. There had been a photograph in the newspaper; but not many people came to watch; there had been no outcry.

But that was in 1962, the last year of Mr. Nehru as father figure, the last year of post-Independence glory for the Indian middle class, when (until the Chinese war blew away the fantasy) India seemed to have made it and Independence was still seen mainly as a matter of personal dignity, an Indian voice abroad, "Indianization" at home, a new kind of job, a managership, an appointment in the new diplomatic service, a new glamour, a conscious display of national costume and "culture."

The lady who in 1975 was so sad, contemplating the tragedy of India, resenting visitors as voyeurs, would in those days have dismissed the subject of Indian poverty; she would have spoken—as middle-class ladies did then—of the happiness of the poor (greater than the happiness of others), their manners, their dignity, the way they kept their hovels clean; she would have contrasted the Indian poor with the unspeakable slum-dwellers of foreign countries. Times had changed. "Indianization" no longer meant a redistribution of jobs, a sharing-out of the British legacy. It was the slogan of an opposition party, a populist-religious appeal to Hindus, a word of threat to minorities, part of the intellectual confusion, the new insecurity, the blind dredging up of dormant fantasies and obsessions, the great enraged stirring from below.

The lady looked down at the floor, and while her husband walked about and talked, she shook her head slowly, saying "Mmmm." In that position her cheeks drooped; and they aged her, adding to her air of melancholy. She knew a family in the demolished settlement, she said. Poor people, simple people. The man had come down to Delhi from the hills. He had found a job and built his little house on this piece of land. He had brought down his wife, and they had since had four children. He was only thirty. But, poor fellow, what other pleasures did he have? He didn't have TV. He had brought down his brother as well, and the brother had brought down his wife, and they had begun to have their own children. Now that life had been smashed. They had all been thrown out in the rain. In the rain: the government couldn't even wait until the monsoon was over.

But had they really been thrown out just like that? Hadn't they been given notice of some sort? Yes, a year's notice. But what could poor people do? It was also true that those who had registered at that time had been given building plots of their own somewhere else. But what did poor people know about registering? Who was there to help them? And, besides, the new plots were ten miles away. How would people get to work? Buses? Yes, there were buses, but I didn't know the Delhi bus service. It was all melancholy and terrible, especially for the family she knew. Who were they? The man worked for her; he was her servant. She had lost her servant; he had lost his job.

It had taken some time to pull the story out, through the lady's melancholy and her husband's hysteria; and neither the lady nor her husband seemed to understand how depressing it was for a visitor, at a time of a real crisis, to have this personal loss (not yet an established loss: the servant could have got a bicycle) presented as an aspect of the national tragedy.

"I come upon people, both men and women, who seem to enjoy being ill-treated by others. It is an emotional luxury for them to dwell on and speak about their grievances and wallow in self-pity. Among such people conversation means relating what they suffer at the hands of official superiors or inferiors, relatives near or distant." This is what the seventy-nine-year-old Bengali writer Nirad Chaudhuri wrote in 1970, in *To Live or Not to Live*, a handbook for Indians on "living happily with others."

Chaudhuri, beating his own way out of the thicket of Indian attitudes, believes that Indians do not *live*, that they live "unsoundly," to no purpose. "Do we live at all? This would seem an absurd question, for none of us commit suicide, though, to be honest, I would confess that I have come to feel that a large majority of the persons I know should do so, because I cannot see any point in their remaining alive."

It was the effect on me of that Delhi evening. I had gone to that apartment expecting ideas, discussion. I had found no ideas, only obsessions, no discussion, only disingenuous complaint and an invitation to the wallow, the sweet surrender to tragedy.

The traffic noise came through the windows and I had to strain to hear what was being said. The lights were very dim and I had to strain to see. It was a government apartment in a suburb far from the central "garden city" of New Delhi. It hadn't been easy to find because, like many places in the suburbs of New Delhi, where streets can be nameless, it had a number rather than a guiding address. And it was numbered like a civil-service file, and had that quality of being worn and much handled and about to be passed on. Our host, a civil servant, high in the service but embittered, connected with a department which was without the resources to do what its name suggested, had very soon detached himself from us. He left his plain wife and bespectacled adolescent son—old error, new hope—to sit with us while, standing in gloomy corners, shielding his prey of the evening from our sight, like an animal eating in secret, he worried and importuned a minor—and exceedingly stupid—provincial politician. The ambition was like despair; it shrieked more than the hysteria of the opposition man who feared arrest and the wallow of the woman who had lost her servant.

My taxi-driver that evening was a Sikh. He had been a sportsman in his time and still had the sportsman's presence. He knew foreign countries by the sportsmen they produced, and he spoke English well; he was a diligent reader of the newspapers. He owned his taxi and had a place in the taxi rank of the hotel. I thought he was better off than most people in India. But his thoughts were of migration. He wanted to go to one of the Arab gulf states. He had paid a large sum of money to a middleman, a "contractor." His papers were almost in order now, he said; all he was waiting for, from the contractor, was his "no objection" certificate. Yet the thought of the large sum he had paid to the contractor worried him. He spoke like a man who knew he had waited too long and had begun to fear that he had been cheated.

For so many people India seemed to have gone wrong; so many people in independent India had become fugitives or sought that status. And this was in Delhi, a migrant city in the better-off north, where people were awakened and energetic, and for whom India ought to have gone right. The land stretched a thousand miles to the east and the south, through the overpopulated Gangetic plain and the rock plateau of the Deccan. At the end of that bad evening it seemed barely imaginable—the huts of the landless along the Poona-Bombay road, the child laborers of Bihar among the blond hanks of jute, the chawls and squatters' settlements in central Bombay, the starved squatters in bright cotton slipping in and out of the stone ruins of Vijayanagar, the famine-wasted bodies just outside Jaipur City. It was like a calamity that no one could come to terms with. I

was without the Indian defenses, which were also the attitudes that contributed to the calamity. I could only wait
for the morning.

2

An immovable government, one-party rule, a democratic
system which engaged only a fraction of the population, a
decadent Gandhianism expressed in the white homespun
of the Congress politician, no longer the sign of service but
the uniform of power, the very sight of which could enrage,
and now the Emergency, a censored press, secret arrests:
it was easy to enter into the hysteria of the opposition
man.

But it was also easy to understand why the revolution
had evaporated. The leaders, offering what they saw as
unassailable Gandhian truths, offering themselves as so
many Gandhis, were misled by the apparent answering
fervor of the crowds. But the India of 1975 was not the
India of 1930 and the Dandi Salt March. Political action
couldn't be concentrated in a single symbolic act (picking
up a handful of salt from the shore at Dandi), a religious
act, a ritual cleansing of a subject and defiled land. The
needs of 1975 were more worldly and difficult. India wasn't
to be cleansed again; it was (as Mrs. Gandhi intuited) to
be cleaned up and got going; it was to be seen to be offering
worldly opportunities. The very fierceness of the Emergency
answered the public mood, assuaged old frustrations. The
crowds went home in peace.

And the Gandhianism of a man like Mr. Desai was as
exhibitionist and hollow as the Gandhianism of the men
he opposed; it offered nothing. The sacrifice was for others

(those corpses outside Mrs. Gandhi's house); Mr. Desai (according to that interview he gave to the foreign journalist) saw himself as secure, immune even from arrest. The revolution was an expression of rage and rejection; but it was a revolution without ideas. It was an emotional outburst, a wallow; it would not have taken India forward; and the revolutionary crowds knew that. At its core, absurdly elevated to a political program, was a subtle distortion of the old Gandhian call to action. At its core were the old Indian attitudes of defeat, the idea of withdrawal, a turning away from the world, a sinking back into the past, the rediscovery of old ways, "simplicity."

Simplicity: it was the obsession that evening in Delhi of the opposition man, and it made discussion impossible. Simplicity was the old India and Gandhi. It was the opposite of everything that independent India had committed itself to, and as a motive for political-moral protest was inexhaustible. Everything that had been done was wrong; nothing was right. The opposite of simplicity was the power politics that had come to India; the opposite of simplicity was repression, concentration camps, Hitler. This was the direction in which India was going, and it was better for this India to be smashed into little bits. Czechoslovakia was a small country: had Czechoslovakia suffered? This view of recent history was startling. But he was a wounded man; and his Gandhian simplicity—like Mr. Desai's—had become indistinguishable from a primitivist rage.

His simplicity was something that could be defined only by negatives. It was a turning away from the idea of the modern state. (Defense? Who would or could conquer India? And this from a responsible man, a maker of opinion, in just the twenty-ninth year of full Indian Independence, after a thousand years of invasions and conquests!) Sim-plicity was, above all, a turning away from the idea of industrial development, the idea of the machine. The Gandhian spinning wheel and the handloom would have saved the peasantry and kept India secure in its villages. (Such engineering effort, though, such a need of electrical power, such organization, such a network of brick-lined canals, to take drinking water for the first time in history to the desert villages of Haryana in the north: and not water for every dwelling—that was impossible—but one or two standpipes per village.)

But perhaps this idea of simplicity—though backed up in the Indian way by quotations from Western sources, and presented as a basis for political action—was something more debilitated, something older. Perhaps it was no more than a turning away from the difficulties of a development that had been seen to be impossible, a consequent intellec-tual surrender, a religious giving up, a yielding to old Indian fantasy: the mystical sense of the Indian past, the idea of eternal India forever spontaneously having its rebirth and growth, the conversion of the destitution and serfdom of rural India (and the heavy-footed vultures squabbling in the rain over the bloated carcasses of dead animals) into a memory of pastoral: a memory of the time, so recent, just out of reach, when people knew the undefiled gods, and the gods gave brahmins all the answers, and the bull drew the plough and the cow gave milk, and the manure of these animals enriched the fields, and the stalks of the harvest thatched the simple huts of the pure.

That Indian past! That fantasy of wholeness and purity, confusing the present! Indian opposition groups in London have circulated a text of the speech Jaya Prakash Narayan delivered the evening before his arrest. It is quite different in tone from the pious venom of Mr. Desai's interview that same day with a foreign journalist. The Narayan speech explains and informs; it is the speech of a constitutionalist who has assembled his facts and references; it quotes the Indian Supreme Court judges and Sir Ivor Jennings. But it is also the speech of an Indian political campaigner addressing a mass audience; and there is a philosophical-historical passage which has to be quoted in full.

> The youth, the peasants, the working class, all with one voice must declare that we will not allow fascism to raise its head in our country. We will not have dictatorship in our country. We will carry on our people's government. This is not Bangladesh. This is not Pakistan. This is Bharat. We have our ancient tradition. Thousands of years ago we had small village republics. That sort of history is behind us. There were village Panchayats in virtually every village. In the times of the Mauryas, Guptas, the Pathan, the Mughals, the Peshwas, we had our Panchayats. The British deliberately broke this tradition in order to strengthen their own hold on the country. This ancient tradition was in Bangladesh and in Pakistan, but they seem to have given it up. But our leaders sought a reawakening. Gandhiji always said that *Swaraj* means *Ramraj*. Swaraj means that every village will have its own rule. Every village, every mohalla and town will manage its own affairs. What they must not do is just hand over the lot to their representatives to get it all done at a "higher level."

The passage that begins with an antifascist call (and gives India a working class, almost as if to equip it for that modern struggle) quickly becomes less straightforward.

India becomes the ancient and sacred land of Bharat, and its past is mystically invoked: leaping the defilement of the British period, the speaker looks back to the eighteenth-century Maratha bandit kings, glances at the Moslem conquerors (the Mughal, the Pathan), jumps a thousand years to the purely Indian Guptas (A.D. 320–600), and goes back a further five hundred years to the Mauryas (322–185 B.C.). Through all this—empires, achievement, chaos, conquest, plunder, the steady loss of Indian territory to the world of Islam—India is said to have kept her soul, to have preserved the democratic ways of her village republics, her "people's government." Democracy hasn't come to India from an alien source; India has had it all along. To rediscover democracy, India has only to rediscover herself.

But then Narayan turns this rediscovery into something more mysterious. "Gandhiji always said that *Swaraj* means *Ramraj*." *Swaraj* means self-rule, self-government; it was the word used in the British days for Indian Independence. *Ramraj* is something else. It is Rama's rule, a fantasy of bliss. Rama is the hero of the *Ramayana*, the sacred Hindu epic. This epic echoes events of 1000 B.C., was composed or set down (by a named poet) at about the same time as the *Aeneid*, but (unlike the *Aeneid*) has always been a living poem, more than literature, possessed by all Hindus, however illiterate or depressed, from childhood. Rama incarnates all the Hindu Aryan virtues; he is at once a man and God; his rule—after exile and sorrow—is the rule of God on earth. The narrative of his adventures fills the imagination of the child; and no Hindu can forget that early closeness to figures and events he later learns to be divine, to be legend and not legend.

Ramraj is something the Hindu always knows he has

lost: in one way remote, impossible, just a word, in another way only as remote as childhood, just out of reach. From *Punjabi Century* (1963), the autobiography of one of India's most distinguished business administrators, Prakash Tandon, we can get a fuller idea of the *Ramraj* Gandhi offered in 1919, at the start of his Indian agitation, and of the political effect then, at a time of high emotion, even on a professional family. "These visitors," Tandon writes,

> spoke about the freedom of India, and this intrigued us: but when they talked in familiar analogies and idiom about the Kal Yug, we saw what they meant. Had it not been prophesied that there were seven eras in India's life and history: there had been a Sat Yug, the era of truth, justice, and prosperity; and then there was to be a Kal Yug, an era of falsehood, of demoralization, of slavery and poverty. . . . Gandhi rechristened India Bharat Mata, a name that evoked nostalgic memories, and associated with Gao Mata, the mother cow. . . . He . . . spoke about the peace of the British as the peace of slavery. Gradually a new picture began to build in our minds, of India coming out of the Kal Yug into a new era of freedom and plenty, Ram Rajya.

Nearly sixty years later, in 1975, Jaya Prakash Narayan's appeal is the same. "*Swaraj* means *Ramraj*." We have gone far beyond the Indian "working class" and the antifascist struggle, beyond political systems and the contemplation of the past; we have gone back to the beginning of the Hindu world, to "nostalgic memories." We have gone back to the solace of incantation, and back to Gandhi as to the only Indian truth. As though Britain still ruled in India; as though Gandhi hadn't been created by specific circumstances; as though the Indian political situation remains unchanging, as eternal as India itself, requiring always the same ideal solution. The irony is that the Indian tyranny against which Jaya Prakash Narayan is protesting, and the sterility of contemporary Indian political life—immovable power on one side, and on the other side frustrated and obsessional "Gandhian" protest, mixing political and historical fantasy with religious exaltation—the irony is that both tyranny and political sterility were ensured by the very success of Gandhi.

It was Gandhi who gave the Congress Party a mass base, a rural base. Four out of five Indians live in villages; and the Congress remains the only party in India (except for certain regional parties) which has a rural organization; it cannot lose. The opposition parties, even a revivalist Hindu party like the Jan Sangh, the National Party, are city parties. In the villages the Congress is still Gandhi's party; and the village tyrannies that have been established through nearly thirty years of unbroken Congress rule cannot now be easily removed. In the countryside the men to watch for are the men in white Gandhian homespun. They are the men of power, the politicians; their authority, rooted in the antique reverences of caste and clan, has been ennobled by Independence and democracy.

Like the two who were introduced to me, late one afternoon, at a great irrigation scheme in the south, as "farmers." I had asked—after lunch and visits to offices and viewing points—to visit fields and see farmers; and the irrigation administrator, in spite of his jacket and tie (emblems of his high administrative rank), became nervous, like a man fearful of trespassing. The ragged men gathering silently around us, obviously connected with the work of the land, were not farmers, as I had thought. What were they? They were laborers, less than laborers, nothing; the administrator seemed not to see them. A government jeep was sent to get the two farmers the administrator said he knew; and we waited for a long time in a damp timber yard, in the dying light of a rainy, overcast day, the crowd around us growing, until the farmers arrived, men in their early fifties, hopping nimbly off the jeep in full Congress uniform of white Gandhian homespun, one man freshly bathed and speaking fluent English and with a big wristwatch, the other man tall and pale and paunchy, with a Gandhi cap: not farmers at all, but landowners and politicians, rulers of the district, acting out for the visitor the democratic charade of being farmers and living each man off the income of six acres of land: taking me, after all that waiting, just across the road from the timber yard to a small, overirrigated field, now in darkness, where their white homespun yet glowed: around us the serfs, underfed, landless, nothing, less than people, dark wasted faces and dark rags fading into the dusk.

To make democracy work, Jaya Prakash Narayan suggests, to undo tyranny, it is only necessary for India to return truly to itself. The *Ramraj* that Gandhi offered is no longer simply Independence, India without the British; it is people's government, the reestablishment of the ancient Indian village republic, a turning away from the secretariats of Delhi and the state capitals. But this is saying nothing; this is to leave India where it is. What looks like a political program is only clamor and religious excitation. People's government and that idea of the ancient Indian village republic (which may be a fanciful idea, a nationalist myth surviving from the days of the Independence struggle) are not the same thing. Old India has its special cruelties; not all the people are people. And (though Narayan doesn't seem aware of the contradiction) it is really against that old India that, later in his speech, he protests.

> She [Mrs. Gandhi] speaks of the welfare of the Harijans [untouchables]. Does she not feel any shame for all the misdeeds done recently to the Harijans? In U.P. [Uttar Pradesh, Mrs. Gandhi's home state] and in Bihar [Narayan's home state] whole Harijan villages have been put to the torch. One Harijan was burnt alive. She does not have any right to speak on behalf of the Harijans. Those poor people, they do not understand all the sophisticated talk. Recently I was in the Bhojpur area. How many Harijans were mercilessly butchered!

India is to be returned to itself, to surrender to its inmost impulses; at the same time India is to be saved from itself. The synthesis of Marxism and Gandhianism which Jaya Prakash Narayan is thought by his admirers to have achieved is in fact a kind of nonsense; he offers as politics a version of an old religious exaltation; and it has made him part of the sterility he is protesting against.

A passionate Marxist journalist—waiting for the revolution, rejecting all "palliatives"—told me that the "workers" of India had to be politicized; they had to be told that it was the "system" that oppressed them. After nearly thirty years of power the Congress has, understandably, become the system. But where does the system begin and end? Does it take in religion, the security of caste and clan, Indian ways of perceiving, karma, the antique serfdom? But no Indian cares to take political self-examination that far. No Indian can take himself to the stage where he might perceive that the faults lie within the civilization itself, that the failure and the cruelties of India might implicate all Indians. Even the Marxists, dreaming of a revolution occurring like magic on a particular day, of tyranny swept away, of "the people" then engaging in the pleasures of "folk" activities—the Marxist journalist's word: the folk miraculously whole after the millennia of oppression—even the Marxists' vision of the future is not of a country undone and remade but of an India essentially returned to itself, purified: a vision of *Ramraj*.

An extraordinary feature of Indian opposition right-wing parties in exile has been their insistence on the antiquity and glory of India. In April 1976, in London, at an "International Conference on Restoration of Democracy in India," the audience heard that Alexander the Great, on his march into India (327 B.C.), had not defeated King Porus of the Punjab. Western histories had lied for two thousand years: Porus had defeated Alexander and compelled him to retreat. Half true about Alexander in India; but the topic, in the circumstances, was unexpected. Yet it was in character. In the program booklet for the conference an Indian merchant in the Dutch West Indies (secure in someone else's economy and political system, the creation of another civilization) had taken space to print this quotation from Swami Vivekananda, the Vedantist who at the turn of the century exported Hinduism to the United States.

Our Punya-Bhumi and its Glorious Past. If there is any land on this earth that can lay claim to be blessed Punya-Bhumi, to be the land to which souls on this earth must come to account for Karma, the land to which every soul that is wending its way Godward must come to attain its last home, the land where humanity has attained its highest towards gentleness, towards calmness, above all, the land of introspection and of spirituality—it is INDIA.

Protest! The restoration of democracy!

"To be critical and not be swept away in a flood of archaic emotions is a much greater effort for us Indians (and I include myself)," Dr. Sudhir Kakar, the psychotherapist at Jawaharlal Nehru University in New Delhi, writes in a recent letter. "The Indian intellectual's struggle is on two fronts—inner and outer—for it has been our developmental fate that, in contrast to say France or Germany, it has always been earliest childhood that was seen to be the golden period of individual life history, just as the remotest past is considered to be the golden age of Indian history."

So, in all the distress of India (now a fact of life, and immutable), protest looks back to the past, to what is thought to have been violated, what is known to be lost. Like childhood, this golden Indian past is not to be possessed by inquiry; it is only to be ecstatically contemplated. The past is a religious idea, clouding intellect and painful perception, numbing distress in bad times. And it is into this past—achingly close in the heart—that Gandhi has been absorbed. He too has become part of what India has lost; he is himself the object of nostalgic memories. To possess him, or to act in his name, is to have the illusion of regaining purity and the past; and in order to possess him, men have only to look inward. Everyone in India is Gandhian; everyone has his own idea of Gandhianism, as everyone has his own intimation of the *Ramraj* he offered.

3

In 1971, after she split the Congress, Mrs. Gandhi called a midterm election. I followed this election in one constituency, Ajmer, in the semidesert state of Rajasthan. The candidate standing against Mrs. Gandhi's man was a blind old Congressman who had taken part in the Independence struggle and had gone to jail. He was a little vain of having gone to jail, and spoke as though the young people coming up who hadn't gone to jail (and couldn't have, because the British had gone away) couldn't be said to have "a record of service."

He was a Gandhian and he wore his elegant homespun and he was honored and he was a man of the utmost probity, and quite rich too, as a lawyer specializing in land-revenue cases. He told me that poor peasants sought him out from all over the state. His record as a legislator after Independence was blameless but null, though he thought that his stand on matters like cow-protection could bear examination by anyone; and he said he had also been connected with a campaign for the correct labeling of certain cooking oils. If he hadn't done more, it was perhaps because he didn't see that there was more for him to do; his main duty was, as it were, to keep the Gandhian prayer wheel turning.

Rajasthan is a state of famine and drought, and it had just been scourged by an eight-year drought; parts of the state had been stripped of trees and turned to desert. But during his campaign (or what I saw of it) the old Congressman made no promises to anybody, and offered no ideas; all he offered was himself and his Gandhianism and his record of service. (There were, it should be said, many complex caste matters to be straightened out.)

I asked him one day, as we were racing across the desert in his campaign jeep, what it was about Gandhi that he particularly admired. He said without hesitation that he admired Gandhi for going to Buckingham Palace in 1931 in a dhoti; that act "put the picture of poor India before the world." As though the world didn't know. But to the old Congressman India's poverty was a very special thing, and I got the impression that, as a Gandhian, he didn't want to see anyone spoiling it. The old man disliked machines; he told me he had heard that people in the West had begun to turn against them as well; and—though in a famine region, and though asking people for votes—he strongly disapproved of having piped water and electricity taken to the villages. Piped water and electricity were "morally bad," especially for the village women. They would be denied valuable "exercise" and become "sluggish," and their health would suffer. No more fetching "healthy water from the well"; no more corn-grinding with the old-fashioned quern. The good old ways were going; everything was being Westernized.

The old Congressman lost the election, and lost it badly. The reason was simple. He had no organization; the local Congress organization (which he had once manipulated) was solidly behind Mrs. Gandhi and her candidate. The old man had forgotten about that. On the afternoon the results were announced I went to see him. He was sitting on a string bed in his drawing room, dressed in white, grieving, supported in his loss by a few silent followers sitting flat on the terrazzo floor. After decades of power, he had been overthrown. And in his defeat the old Congressman saw the death of Gandhian India, the India where, as he defined it, people believed that "means should be as fair as the end."

"There are no morals now," the old man said. "The Machiavellian politics of Europe have begun to touch our own politics and we will go down."

Blind to his own political nullity, the idle self-regard of his own Gandhian concept of service, he was yet half right about India, for a reason he would not have understood. "Archaic emotions," "nostalgic memories": when these were awakened by Gandhi, India became free. But the India created in this way had to stall. Gandhi took India out of one kind of *Kal Yug*, one kind of Black Age; his success inevitably pushed it back into another.

8
Renaissance or Continuity?

1

Gandhi lived too long. Returning to India from South Africa in 1915, at the age of forty-five, holding himself aloof from the established politicians of the time, involving himself with communities and groups hitherto untouched by politics, taking up purely local causes here and there (a land tax, a mill strike), he then very quickly, from 1919 to 1930, drew all India together in a new kind of politics.

Not everyone approved of Gandhi's methods. Many were dismayed by the apparently arbitrary dictates of his "inner voice." And in the political stalemate of the 1930s— for which some Indians still blame him: Gandhi's unpredictable politics, they say, his inability to manage the forces he had released, needlessly lengthened the Independence struggle, delayed self-government by twenty-five years, and wasted the lives and talents of many good men—in the 1930s the management of Indian politics passed into other hands.

Gandhi himself (like Tolstoy, his early inspiration) declined into a long and ever more private mahatmahood. The obsessions were always made public, but they were personal, like his—again almost Tolstoyan—sexual anxieties in old age, after forty years of abstinence. This period of decline was the period of his greatest fame; so that, even while he lived, "he became his admirers." He became his emblems, his holy caricature, the object of competitive piety. Knowledge of the man as a man was lost; mahatmahood submerged all the ambiguities and the political creativity of his early years, the modernity (in India) of so much of his thought. He was claimed in the end by old India, that very India whose political deficiencies he had seen so clearly, with his South African eye.

What was new about him then was not the semi-religious nature of his politics; that was in the Indian tradition. What made him new was the nature of the battles he had fought in South Africa. And what was most revolutionary and un-Indian about him was what he left unexpressed and what perhaps, as an Indian, he had no means of expressing: his racial sense, the sense of belonging to a people specifically of the Indian subcontinent, that the twenty years in South Africa had taught him.

The racial sense is alien to Indians. Race is something they detect about others, but among themselves they know only the subcaste or caste, the clan, the gens, the language group. Beyond that they cannot go; they do not see themselves as belonging to an Indian race; the words have no meaning. Historically, this absence of cohesiveness has been the calamity of India. In South Africa, as Gandhi soon saw, it was the great weakness of the small Indian community, embattled but fragmented, the wealthy Gujarati Moslem merchants calling themselves "Arabs," the Indian Christians claiming only their Christianity, both separating themselves from the indentured laborers of Madras and Bihar, all subjected as Indians to the same racial laws.

If it was in London as a law student that Gandhi decided that he was a Hindu by conviction, it was in South Africa that he added to this the development of a racial consciousness, that consciousness without which a disadvantaged or persecuted minority can be utterly destroyed, and which with Gandhi in South Africa was like an extension of his religious sense: teaching responsibility and compassion, teaching that no man was an island, and that the dignity of the high was bound up with the dignity of the low.

"His Hindu nationalism spoils everything," Tolstoy had said of Gandhi in 1910, while Gandhi was still in South Africa. It is obvious in Gandhi's autobiography, this growing, un-Indian awareness of an Indian group identity. It is there in his early dismay at the indifference of the Gujarati merchants to proposed anti-Indian legislation; in his shock at the appearance in his office of an indentured Tamil laborer who had been beaten up by his employer; and the shock and dismay are related to his own humiliations during his first journey to Pretoria in 1893, when he was twenty-three. Gandhi never forgot that night journey to Pretoria; more than thirty years later he spoke of it as the turning point of his life. But the racial theme is never acknowledged as such in the autobiography. It is always blurred over by religious self-searching, "experiments with truth," attempts at the universal; though for twenty years, until early middle age, he was literally a racial leader, fighting racial battles; and it was as a racial leader that he returned to India, an oddity among the established politicians, to whom "Indian" was only a word, each man with his own regional or caste power base.

Indians were not a minority in India; racial politics of the sort Gandhi knew in South Africa would not have been understood. And at least some of the ambiguities of his early days in India can be traced back to his wish to repeat his South African racial-religious experience, to get away from the divisive politics of religion and caste and region: his seemingly perverse insistence that India was not ready for self-government, that India had to purge itself of its own injustices first, his mystical definitions of self-government, his emphasis on the removal of untouchability, his support of trivial Moslem issues in order to draw Moslems and Hindus together.

He had no means, in India, of formulating the true racial lessons of South Africa; and perhaps he couldn't have done so, any more than he could have described what he had seen as a young man in London in 1888. The racial message always merged into the religious one; and it involved him in what looked like contradictions (against untouchability, but not against the caste system; a passionate Hindu, but preaching unity with the Moslems). The difficult lessons of South Africa were simplified and simplified in India: ending as a holy man's fad for doing the latrine-cleaning work of untouchables, seen only as an exercise in humility, ending as a holy man's plea for brotherhood and love, ending as nothing.

In the 1930s the Moslems fell away from Gandhi and

turned to their own Moslem leaders, preaching the theory of two nations. In 1947 the country was partitioned, and many millions were killed and many more millions expelled from their ancestral land: as great a holocaust as that caused by Nazi Germany. And in 1948 Gandhi was killed by a Hindu for having undermined and betrayed Hindu India. Irony upon irony; but the South African Indian had long ago been lost in the Hindu mahatma; and mahatma-hood in the end had worked against his Indian cause.

Jamnalal Bajaj, a pious Hindu of a northern merchant caste, was one of Gandhi's earliest financial backers in India. He gave the land and the money for the famous ashram Gandhi founded at Wardha, a village chosen be-cause it was in the center of India. Bajaj died in 1942; and his widow, honoring his memory, gave away a lot of money to cow-protection societies. Ved Mehta recently went to interview the old lady for his book *Mahatma Gandhi and His Apostles*. After Gandhi's death in 1948, Mrs. Bajaj said, she had transferred her loyalty to Vinoba Bhave, the man recognized as Gandhi's successor. "I walked with Vinobaji for years," Mrs. Bajaj told Mehta. "Ten or fifteen miles a day, begging land for the poor. It was very hard, changing camp every day, because I never eat anything I haven't prepared with my own hands. Everyone knows that Mos-lems and Harijans have dirty habits." And the old lady, who had been chewing something, spat.

But the end was contained in the beginning. "For me there can be no deliverance from this earthly life except in India. Anyone who seeks such deliverance . . . must go to the sacred soil of India. For me, as for everyone else, the land of India is the 'refuge of the afflicted.' " This pas-sage—which is quoted by Judith M. Brown in her study of

Gandhi's entry into Indian politics, *Gandhi's Rise to Power* (1972)—comes from an article Gandhi wrote for his South African paper in 1914, at the very end of his time in South Africa, just before he returned to India by way of England. After the racial battles, the South African leader, with his now developed antipathy to Western industrial civilization, was returning to India as to the Hindu holy land: even at the beginning, then, he was already too various, and people had to find in him what they wanted to find, or what they could most easily grasp.

Judith Brown quotes a letter to a relative, written a few months before the newspaper article: "The real secret of life seems to consist in so living in the world as it is, without being attached to it, that *moksha* [salvation, absorption into the One, freedom from rebirth] might become easy of attainment to us and to others. This will include service of self, the family, the community, and the State." This declaration of faith, apparently a unity, conceals at least four personalities. The Hindu dreams of nonattachment and salvation; the man exposed to Western religious thought thinks that the conduct of the individual should also make salvation easy for others; the South African Indian preaches the widest social loyalty (the community, the Indian community); the political campaigner, with his respect for (and dependence on) British law and institutions, stresses service to the state.

It was too much. Something of this complex South African ideology had to go in the holy land of India; and many things went. The racial intimations remained unexpressed; and what was utterly consumed—by holiness, the subjection of India, the lengthening of the Independence struggle, and the mahatma's hardening antipathy to the machine, at once the symbol of oppression and the West—what was utterly consumed was that intrusive and unmanageable idea of service to the state.

For Vinoba Bhave, Gandhi's successor in independent India, the Gandhian ideal is the "withering away" of the state. Or so he said many years ago. What does it mean, the withering away of the state? It means nothing. It means this: "Our first step will be to get Gram-Raj [government by the village]: then lawsuits and disputes will be judged and settled within the village. Next it will be Ram-Raj [the Kingdom of God]: then there will no longer be any lawsuits or disputes, and we shall all live as one family." Bhave said that more than twenty years ago (the quotation is from an admiring biography by an Italian, published in London in 1956). And something like that is still being said by others today, in the more desperate circumstances of the Emergency. "Wanted: a Gandhian Constitution" is the title of a recent article in the *Illustrated Weekly of India*, which, since the Emergency, has been running a debate about the Indian constitution. The writer, a former state governor and ambassador, merely makes the plea for village government; he also takes the occasion to talk about his acquaintance with Gandhi; and the article is illustrated by a photograph of the writer and his wife sitting on the floor and using a quern, grinding their daily corn together in pious idleness.

It is what Gandhianism was long ago reduced to by the mahatmahood: religious ecstasy and religious self-display, a juggling with nothing, a liberation from constructive thought and political burdens. True freedom and true piety are still seen to lie in withdrawal from the difficult world.

In independent India, Gandhianism is like the solace still of a conquered people, to whom the state has historically been alien, controlled by others.

Perhaps the only politician with something of Gandhi's racial sense and his feeling for all-India was Nehru, who, like Gandhi, was somewhat of a displaced person in India. At first they look so unalike; but only twenty years lay between the mahatma and the English-educated Nehru; and both men were made by critical years spent outside India. In his autobiography Nehru says he was infected by the prevailing, and fashionable, anti-Semitism at Harrow School; he could hardly have failed there to have become aware of his Indianness.

The irony is that in independent India the politicians who have come up are not far removed from the men whom Gandhi—short-circuiting the established Western-style politicians of the time—began to draw into politics in 1917. They are small-town men, provincials, and they remain small because their power is based on the loyalties of caste and region. The idea of all-India is not always within their grasp. They have spoken instead, since the 1960s, only of India's need for "emotional integration"; and the very words speak of fracture. The racial sense, which contains respect for the individual and even that concept of "the people," remains as remote from India as ever. So that even Marxism tends to be only its jargon, a form of mimicry: "the people" so often turn out to be people of a certain region and of a certain caste.

Gandhi swept through India, but he has left it without an ideology. He awakened the holy land; his mahatmahood returned it to archaism; he made his worshipers vain.

2

Vinoba Bhave, Gandhi's successor, is more a mascot than a mahatma. He is in the old Indian tradition of the sage who lives apart from men, but not so far from them that they are unable to provide him with a life-support system. Before such a sage the prince prostrates himself, in order to be reminded of the eternal verities. The prince visiting the sage: it is a recurring theme in Indian painting, from both Hindu and Moslem courts. The prince, for all his finery, is the suppliant; the sage, ash-smeared or meager with austerities or bursting with his developed inner life, sits serenely outside his hut or below a tree. There is no particular wisdom that the sage offers; he is important simply because he is there. And this is the archaic role— one or two centuries away from Gandhi in South Africa in 1893, Gandhi in India in 1917—that Bhave has created for himself in contemporary India, as Gandhi's successor. He is not a particularly intelligent man and, as a perfect disciple of the mahatma, not original; his political views come close to nonsense. But he is very old; something of the aura of the dead mahatma still hangs about him; and he is the man the politicians would like to have on their side.

For some time in the 1950s Bhave was associated with Jaya Prakash Narayan, who later became one of the opposition leaders. And there was some anxiety, when the Emergency was declared in June 1975 and Narayan was arrested, about what Bhave would say. But, as it happened, Bhave wasn't talking at the time. It was the mahatma's custom, in later years, to have a weekly day of silence. Bhave, in emulation of the mahatma, but always overdoing things, had imposed a whole year's silence on himself; and there were still some months of this silence to go. Eventually, however, it was reported that various statements had been shown the old man—in the manner of those questionnaires that call for the ticking of boxes—and he had made some signs to indicate his support for the suspension of the constitution and the declaration of the state of Emergency.

When, later, he fell ill, Mrs. Gandhi flew to see him; and her personal physician gave him a check-up. It was Mrs. Gandhi who, under heavy security, spoke at the meeting held in Delhi to honor Bhave's eightieth birthday; and it was in deference to Bhave—or so I heard it said—that, in all the uncertainty of the Emergency, Mrs. Gandhi reproclaimed the prohibition of alcohol as one of the goals of the government. Six doctors in the meantime were looking after the old sage; thus cosseted, he lived through his year of silence and at last, in January 1976, he spoke. The time had come, he said, for India to move from rule by the majority to rule by unanimity. Which was quite astute for a man of eighty. The actual statement didn't mean much; but it showed that he was still interested, that India was still protected by his sanctity.

Bhave in himself is nothing, a medieval throwback of whom there must be hundreds or thousands in India. But he is important because he is now all that India has as a moral reference, and because for the last thirty years he has been, as it were, the authorized version of Gandhi. He has fixed the idea of Gandhianism for India. In spite of the minute documentation of the life, in spite of the studies and the histories, it is unlikely that in the Indian mind—with its poor historical sense, its capacity for myth—Gandhi will ever be more than Bhave's magical interpretation of him.

When the politicians now, on one side or the other, speak of Gandhi or Gandhianism, they really mean Bhave. By a life of strenuous parody Bhave has swallowed his master. Gandhi took the vow of sexual abstinence when he was thirty-seven, after a great struggle. Bhave took the same vow when he was a child. It has been his way: in his parody all the human complexity of the mahatma has been dimmed into mere holiness. Bhave has from the start looked for salvation in simple obedience alone. But by obeying what in his simplicity he has understood to be the rules, by exaggerating the mahatma's more obvious gestures, he has become something older even than the mahatma in his last phase.

Gandhi was made by London, the study of the law, the twenty years in South Africa, Tolstoy, Ruskin, the *Gita*. Bhave was made only by Gandhi's ashrams and India. He went to the Ahmedabad ashram when he was very young. He worked in the kitchens, in the latrines, and sat for such long hours at the spinning wheel that Gandhi, fearing for the effect of this manual zeal on the young man's mind, sent him away to study. He studied for a year in the holy city of Banaras. Lanza del Vasto, Bhave's Italian biographer (*Gandhi to Vinoba: the New Pilgrimage*, 1956), gives some idea of the magical nature of these studies:

It is . . . certain that he consulted some hermit on the banks of the Ganges on contemplation and concentration, the suspension of the breath, the rousing of the Serpent coiled up at the base of the spine, and its ascension through the chakkras to the thousand-petaled lotus at the top of the head; the effacement of the "I" and the discovery of the Self.

At Banaras one day a literature student asked Bhave about *Shakuntala*, the late-fourth-century Sanskrit play by the poet Kalidasa. It was a good subject to raise with someone who knew Sanskrit, because *Shakuntala*, which in translation reads only like a romance of recognition, is considered one of the glories of Sanskrit literature, and comes from what is thought of as a golden age in Indian civilization. But Bhave was fierce with the inquirer. He said, "I have never read the *Shakuntala* of Kalidasa, and I never shall. I do not learn the language of the gods to amuse myself with love stories and literary trifles."

For Bhave's biographer this is part of Bhave's perfection. It is how Indian spirituality, taken to its limits, swallows up and annuls that very civilization of which Indians boast, but of which, generally, they know little. Bhave, in the vanity of his spiritual perfection, is more than a decadent Gandhian. His religion is a kind of barbarism; it would return men to the bush. It is the religion of poverty and dust. And it is not extraordinary that Bhave's ideas about education should be like those of Mr. Squeers. Get the children out into the fields, among the animals: it was, after all, the only education that the god Krishna received.

Bhave's Italian biographer, holidaying away from Europe, can at times get carried away by the Oriental wisdom of his subject, so suited to the encompassing physical wretchedness; and the book is padded out with the master's sayings. (Bhave, though he has published, doesn't believe in writing books: he has to be savored in his sayings.) This is the political Bhave: "The will of the people by itself equals 1. The State by itself equals 0. Together these make 10. Does 10 equal 10 because of the 1 or because of the 0?" And this is Bhave (pre 1956) on the wickedness of the machine: "Are the richest crops gathered in America, where the sowing is done from the air, or in China, where all the land is cultivated by hand on miniature allotments?"

It is hard to imagine now, but in 1952, when newly independent India was taken at its own valuation in many countries, Bhave appeared on the cover of *Time* magazine. The successor to the mahatma, and almost a mahatma himself! This was not long after Bhave had started his "Land Gift" scheme. It was his Gandhian attempt to solve the problem of the Indian landless, and it is the venture with which his name is still associated. His plan was to go about India on foot, to walk and walk, perhaps forever, asking people with land to give some to the landless. The *Time* cover was captioned with a Bhave saying: "I have come to loot you with love."

The idea of the long walk was borrowed from Gandhi. But it was based on a misunderstanding. Gandhi's walks or marches were purely symbolic; they were intended as gestures, theater. In 1930 Gandhi had walked in slow, well-publicized stages from Ahmedabad to the sea, not to do anything big when he got there, but just to pick up salt, in this way breaking an easily breakable law and demonstrating to all India his rejection of British rule. In 1947, in Bengal, he had walked in the Noakhali district, just to show himself, hoping by his presence to stop the communal killings.

These were fairly long walks. But Bhave—as usual—intended his own walk to be much, much longer, to be, it might be said, a career; and he didn't intend it to be symbolic. He was aiming at nothing less than land-redistribution as he skittered through the Indian villages, hoping, by the religious excitement of a day, to do what could (and can) be done only by law, consolidating administration, and years of patient education. It was like an attempt at a Gandhian rope trick: the substitution of spirituality for the machinery of the state. It tied in with Bhave's avowed Gandhian aim of seeing the state "wither away." India, released by Gandhi from subjection, was now to regenerate itself by the same spiritual means. All the other "isms" of the world were to be made obsolete. It was an open, breathtaking experiment in Gandhian magic; and the interest of *Time* magazine, the interest of the West—always important to India, even at its most spiritual—kept the excitement high.

It became fashionable to walk with Bhave. It became, in the words of Lanza del Vasto, "the new pilgrimage." For a few weeks early in 1954 Lanza del Vasto walked with Bhave; and Vasto—Gandhian though he was, with a best-seller about Gandhi under his belt, and hoping to do something with Bhave too—Vasto found the going rough. Even in his awestruck account a European-accented irritation keeps breaking in at the discomforts and disorder of the Bhave march: the bad food, peppery and oversalted; the atmosphere of the circus, the constant noise, the worshiping crowds chattering like aviaries, easily distracted, even in the presence of the master; Bhave's own followers, incapable of talking in anything but shouts, constantly publicly belching and hawking and farting. Vasto tries hard to understand; a prisoner of his pilgrimage, he tries, by a natural association of ideas, to find in the torment of the nightly camp "the innocence of the fart . . . the sportings of a lovable people which loves to communicate."

And every day there is the next village, and the hard clay roads of Bihar. Always, Bhave strides ahead, in the lead. No villager, however worshiping or rapturous, must run across his path or walk in front of him. It is permitted only to follow—sainthood, and the salvation it offers (contained in the mere sight of the saint), has its stringencies. At one stage Bhave, for no apparent reason, seems to have his doubts and seems to be dropping hints of a fast against the "laziness" of some of his staff (which includes a press officer) and the "meanness" of some other people. Clearly, things have been going on behind the scenes that Vasto doesn't know about. But long before then it has occurred to the reader that, in spite of all the sermons, this walk is just a walk; that nothing, or very little, is being done; that none of those chattering villagers may be either giving or getting land; that everybody is just declaring for God.

In the early days there had been talk of a university to serve the special needs of the movement, and someone had given land for it not far from the site of the Buddha's Enlightenment. Bhave was asked about the university one day. He said, "The ground is there and I've had a well dug on it. The passer-by will be able to draw a bucket of water and drink his fill." But the questioner wanted to know about the university. "What will be its aims, statutes, and syllabuses?" Bhave said: "The ground is there, the well is there. Whoever wants to drink will drink. What more do you want?"

Even for a saint, this was living dangerously. But Bhave was Bhave, and it was seven more years before he gave up the long walk and settled down quietly as a sage, sinking into the stupor of meditation.

Magic hadn't worked; spirituality hadn't brought about land-redistribution or, more importantly, the revolution in social attitudes that such a redistribution required. The effect, in fact, had been the opposite. The living saint, officially adulated, preceded by magical reports, offering salvation to all who cast eyes on him, was a living confirmation of the rightness of the old ways, of the necessity for old reverences. Bihar, where Bhave did much of his walking, remains—in matters of land and untouchability—among the most backward and crushed of the Indian states.

Bhave, even if he understood Gandhi's stress on the need for social reform, was incapable of undermining Hindu India; he was too much part of it. The perfect disciple, obeying without always knowing why, he invariably distorted his master's message. Once, on the march, he said that untouchables did work human beings shouldn't do; for that reason they should be given land, to become tillers. This might have seemed Gandhian; but all that the words could be taken to mean was that latrine-cleaners were latrine-cleaners, that untouchables were untouchables. The whole point of Gandhi's message was lost.

Hindu speculation can soar high; but Hindu religious practices are elemental, and spirituality for most people is a tangible good, magic. Bhave offered spirituality as just such a good; and he could offer it as a commodity in which, as Gandhi's heir, he was specially licensed to deal. At a public meeting in 1962—at Shantiniketan, the university founded by the poet Tagore to revive the arts in India—Bhave described himself as "a retailer of spirituality." At Shantiniketan! Such was Bhave's security in India; to such a degree had the rational thought of a man like Tagore been chewed up by the cultural primitivism of Gandhian India.

Some years before, in a memorable statement made

during the great days of the long walk, Bhave had described himself as the fire. It was his duty simply to burn; it was for others to use his fire. Humility, once it becomes a vow, ceases to be humility, Gandhi said in his autobiography; and Bhave's interpretation of his function in India is as vain and decadent as it appears. It was a perversion of the *Gita*'s idea of duty, a perversion of the idea of *dharma*; it was the language of the magician.

Bhave, with his simplicity and distortions, offered Gandhianism as a kind of magic; and he offered himself as the magician. Gandhi, the South African, was too complex for India. India made the racial leader the mahatma; and in Bhave the mahatma became Merlin. He failed, but that did not tarnish his sainthood. He had failed, after all, only because the times were bad; because, as so many Indians say, offering it as the profoundest wisdom, since the death of Gandhi truth has fled from India and the world. In a Black Age, Bhave had virtuously attempted old magic; and on his eightieth birthday he was honored in New Delhi. Paunchy Congressmen in crisp white homespun sat on the platform and some made speeches. Mrs. Gandhi, after a little fumbling, carefully garlanded his portrait.

The latest—censored and incomplete—news about Bhave is that in June 1976 he started a public fast. In this fast, which he must have considered his last public act, there is still the element of Gandhian parody. Gandhi, too, did a famous last fast. But Gandhi's fast—his last expression of pain and despair in partitioned India—was against human slaughter in the Punjab and Bengal. Bhave's last fast, if the reports are correct, was against cow-slaughter.

It seems to be always there in India: magic, the past,

the death of the intellect, spirituality annulling the civilization out of which it issues, India swallowing its own tail.

3

With the dismantling, during the Emergency, of its borrowed or inherited democratic institutions, and with no foreign conqueror now to impose a new order, India for the first time for centuries is left alone with the blankness of its decayed civilization. The freedoms that came to independent India with the institutions it gave itself were alien freedoms, better suited to another civilization; in India they remained separate from the internal organization of the country, its beliefs and antique restrictions. In the beginning it didn't matter. There were development plans. India industrialized, more effectively than is generally supposed; it more than doubled its production of food; it is now the world's fourth largest producer of grain. And out of this prodigious effort arose a new mutinous stirring, which took India by surprise, and with which it didn't know how to cope. It was as though India didn't know what its Independence had committed it to.

The population grew; the landless fled from the tyranny of the villages; the towns choked; the restlessness created by the beginnings of economic development—in a land immemorially abject—expressed itself in the streets, in varying ways. In this very triumph of democracy lay its destruction. Formal politics answered less and less, became more and more formal; toward the end it had the demeanor of a parlor game, and became an affair of head-counting and floor-crossing. And the Indian press, another borrowed institution, also failed. With its restricted view of its function, it matched the triviality of the politics; it became part of the Indian anarchy. It reported speeches and more speeches; it reduced India to its various legislative chambers. It turned into national figures those politicians who were the least predictable; and both they and the freedom of the press vanished with the Emergency.

The dismantled institutions—of law and press and parliament—cannot simply be put together again. They have been undone; they can be undone again; it has been demonstrated that freedom is not an absolute in independent India. Mrs. Gandhi has given her name to the Emergency, and impressed it with her personality. It is unfortunate that this should be so, because it has simplified comment on one side and the other, and blurred the true nature of the crisis. With or without Mrs. Gandhi, independent India—with institutions of government opposed to its social organization, with problems of poverty that every Indian feels in his bones to be beyond solution—would have arrived at a state of emergency. And the Emergency, even with Mrs. Gandhi's immense authority, is only a staying action. However it is resolved, India will at the end be face to face with its own emptiness, the inadequacy of an old civilization which is cherished because it is all men have but which no longer answers their needs.

India is without an ideology—and that was the failure of Gandhi and India together. Its people have no idea of the state, and none of the attitudes that go with such an idea· no historical notion of the past, no identity beyond the tenuous ecumenism of Hindu beliefs, and, in spite of the racial excesses of the British period, not even the beginnings of a racial sense. Through centuries of conquest the civilization declined into an apparatus for survival, turning

away from the mind (on which the sacred *Gita* lays such
stress) and creativity (Vinoba Bhave finding in Sanskrit
only the language of the gods, and not the language of
poets), stripping itself down, like all decaying civilizations,
to its magical practices and imprisoning social forms. To
enable men to survive, men had to be diminished. And
this was a civilization that could narrow and still appear
whole. Perhaps because of its unconcealed origins in racial
conquest (victorious Aryans, subjugated aborigines), it is
shot through with ambiguous beliefs that can either exalt
men or abase them.

The key Hindu concept of *dharma*—the right way, the
sanctioned way, which all men must follow, according to
their natures—is an elastic concept. At its noblest it combines self-fulfillment and truth to the self with the ideas of
action as duty, action as its own spiritual reward, man as
a holy vessel. And it ceases then to be mysterious; it touches
the high ideals of other civilizations. It might be said that
it is of *dharma* that Balzac is writing when, near the end of
his creative life, breaking through fatigue and a long blank
period to write *Cousine Bette* in eight weeks, he reflects on
the artist's vocation:

> Constant labor is the law of art as well as the law of life, for
> art is the creative activity of the mind. And so great artists,
> true poets, do not wait for either commissions or clients;
> they create today, tomorrow, ceaselessly. And there results
> a habit of toil, a perpetual consciousness of the difficulties,
> that keeps them in a state of marriage with the Muse, and
> her creative forces.

And Proust, too, killing himself to write his book, comes
close to the concept of *dharma* when, echoing Balzac, he

says that in the end it is less the desire for fame than "the habit of laboriousness" that takes a writer to the end of a work. But *dharma,* as this ideal of truth to oneself, or living out the truth in oneself, can also be used to reconcile men to servitude and make them find in paralyzing obedience the highest spiritual good. "And do thy duty, even if it be humble," says the Aryan *Gita,* "rather than another's, even if it be great. To die in one's duty is life: to live in another's is death."

Dharma is creative or crippling according to the state of the civilization, according to what is expected of men. It cannot be otherwise. The quality of a faith is not a constant; it depends on the quality of the men who profess it. The religion of a Vinoba Bhave can only express the dust and defeat of the Indian village. Indians have made some contribution to science in this century; but—with a few notable exceptions—their work has been done abroad. And this is more than a matter of equipment and facilities. It is a cause of concern to the Indian scientific community—which feels itself vulnerable in India—that many of those men who are so daring and original abroad should, when they are lured back to India, collapse into ordinariness and yet remain content, become people who seem unaware of their former worth, and seem to have been brilliant by accident. They have been claimed by the lesser civilization, the lesser idea of *dharma* and self-fulfillment. In a civilization reduced to its forms, they no longer have to strive intellectually to gain spiritual merit in their own eyes; that same merit is now to be had by religious right behavior, correctness.

India grieved for the scientist Har Gobind Khorana who, as an American citizen, won a Nobel Prize in medicine

for the United States a few years ago. India invited him
back and feted him; but what was most important about
him was ignored. "We would do everything for Khorana,"
one of India's best journalists said, "except do him the
honor of discussing his work." The work, the labor, the
assessment of that labor: it was expected that somehow
that would occur elsewhere, outside India.

It is part of the intellectual parasitism that Indians
accept (and, as a conquered people, have long accepted)
while continuing to see their civilization as whole and possessed of the only truth that matters: offering refuge to
"the afflicted," as Gandhi saw it in 1914, and "deliverance
from this earthly life." It is as though it is in the very
distress and worldly incapacity of India—rather than in its
once vigorous civilization—that its special virtue has now
to be found. And it is like the solace of despair, because
(as even Gandhi knew, and as all his early political actions
showed) there is no virtue in worldly defeat.

Indian poverty is more dehumanizing than any machine;
and, more than in any machine civilization, men in India
are units, locked up in the straitest obedience by their idea
of their *dharma*. The scientist returning to India sheds the
individuality he acquired during his time abroad; he regains
the security of his caste identity, and the world is once
more simplified. There are minute rules, as comforting as
bandages; individual perception and judgment, which once
called forth his creativity, are relinquished as burdens, and
the man is once more a unit in his herd, his science reduced
to a skill. The blight of caste is not only untouchability
and the consequent deification in India of filth; the blight,
in an India that tries to grow, is also the over-all obedience
it imposes, its ready-made satisfactions, the diminishing

of adventurousness, the pushing away from men of individuality and the possibility of excellence.

Men might rebel; but in the end they usually make their peace. There is no room in India for outsiders. The Arya Samaj, the Aryan Association, a reformist group opposed to traditional ideas of caste, and active in north India earlier in the century, failed for a simple reason. It couldn't meet the marriage needs of its members; India called them back to the castes and rules they had abjured. And five years ago in Delhi I heard this story. A foreign businessman saw that his untouchable servant was intelligent, and decided to give the young man an education. He did so, and before he left the country he placed the man in a better job. Some years later the businessman returned to India. He found that his untouchable was a latrine-cleaner again. He had been boycotted by his clan for breaking away from them; he was barred from the evening smoking group. There was no other group he could join, no woman he could marry. His solitariness was insupportable, and he had returned to his duty, his *dharma*; he had learned to obey.

Obedience: it is all that India requires of men, and it is what men willingly give. The family has its rules; the caste has its rules. For the disciple, the guru—whether holy man or music teacher—stands in the place of God, and has to be implicitly obeyed, even if—like Bhave with Gandhi—he doesn't always understand why. Sacred texts have to be learned by heart; school texts have to be learned by heart, and university textbooks, and the notes of lecturers. "It is a fault in the Western system of education," Vinoba Bhave said some years ago, "that it lays so little stress on learning great lines by heart." And the children of middle schools chant their lessons like Buddhist novices, raising their voices, like the novices, when the visitor appears, to show their zeal. So India ever absorbs the new into its old self, using new tools in old ways, purging itself of unnecessary mind, maintaining its equilibrium. The poverty of the land is reflected in the poverty of the mind; it would be calamitous if it were otherwise.

The civilization of conquest was also the civilization of defeat; it enabled men, obeying an elastic *dharma*, to dwindle with their land. Gandhi awakened India; but the India he awakened was only the India of defeat, the holy land he needed after South Africa.

Like a novelist who splits himself into his characters, unconsciously setting up the consonances that give his theme a closed intensity, the many-sided Gandhi permeates modern India. He is hidden, unknown except in his now moribund Bhave incarnation; but the drama that is being played out in India today is the drama he set up more than sixty years ago, when he returned to India after the racial battles of South Africa. The creator does not have to understand the roots of his obsessions; his duty is merely to set events in motion. Gandhi gave India its politics; he called up its archaic religious emotions. He made them serve one another, and brought about an awakening. But in independent India the elements of that awakening negate one another. No government can survive on Gandhian fantasy· and the spirituality, the solace of a conquered people, which Gandhi turned into a form of national assertion, has soured more obviously into the nihilism that it always was.

The opposition spokesmen in exile speak of the loss of democracy and freedom; and their complaints are just. But the borrowed words conceal archaic Gandhian obsessions as destructive as many of the provisions of the Emergency: fantasies of *Ramraj*, fantasies of spirituality, a return to the village, simplicity. In these obsessions—the cause of political battle—there still live, in the unlikeliest way, the disturbance of Gandhi's blind years in London as a law student and the twenty years' racial wounding in South Africa. They are now lost, the roots of Gandhi's rejection of the West and his nihilism; the failure of the twenty years in South Africa is expunged from the Indian consciousness. But if Gandhi had resolved his difficulties in another way, if (like the imaginative novelist) he hadn't so successfully transmuted his original hurt (which with him must have been in large part racial), if he had projected onto India another code of survival, he might have left independent India with an ideology, and perhaps even with what in India would have been truly revolutionary, the continental racial sense, the sense of belonging to a people specifically of India, which would have answered all his political aims, and more: not only weakening untouchability and submerging caste, but also awakening the individual, enabling men to stand alone within a broader identity, establishing a new idea of human excellence.

Now the people who fight about him fight about nothing; neither he nor old India has the solutions to the present crisis. He was the last expression of old India; he took India to the end of that road. All the arguments about the Emergency, all the references to his name reveal India's intellectual vacuum, and the emptiness of the civilization to which he seemed to give new life.

In conquered India renaissance has always been taken to mean a recovery of what has been suppressed or dishonored, an exalting of old ways; in periods of respite men have never taken the opportunity, or perhaps have been without the intellectual means, to move ahead; and disaster has come again. Art historians tell us that the European renaissance became established when men understood that the past was not living on; that Ovid or Virgil could not be thought of as a kind of ancient cleric; that men had to put distance between the past and themselves, the better to understand and profit from that past. India has always sought renewal in the other way, in continuity. In the earliest texts men look back to the past and speak of the present Black Age; just as they look back now to the days of Gandhi and the fight against the British, and see all that has followed as defilement rather than as the working out of history. While India tries to go back to an idea of its past, it will not possess that past or be enriched by it. The past can now be possessed only by inquiry and scholarship, by intellectual rather than spiritual discipline. The past has to be seen to be dead; or the past will kill.

The stability of Gandhian India was an illusion; and India will not be stable again for a long time. But in the present uncertainty and emptiness there is the possibility of a true new beginning, of the emergence in India of mind, after the long spiritual night. "The crisis of India is not political: this is only the view from Delhi. Dictatorship or rule by the army will change nothing. Nor is the crisis only economic. These are only aspects of the larger crisis, which is that of a decaying civilization, where the only hope lies in further swift decay." I wrote that in 1967; and that seemed to me a blacker time.

August 1975—October 1976

VIDIADHAR SURAJPRASAD NAIPAUL was born on August 17, 1932, in the small town of Chaguanas, Trinidad. Raised as a Hindu by his Indian parents, Naipaul left the island at the age of eighteen to attend Oxford University on a scholarship. His first three books, *The Mystic Masseur*, *The Suffrage of Elvira*, and *Miguel Street* were followed in 1961 by the publication of *A House for Mr. Biswas*, acclaimed by critics as a masterpiece and considered by Naipaul himself to be the work that marked his transition to maturity as a writer. He has since written many other works of fiction and non-fiction, including *The Overcrowded Barracoon*, *The Loss of El Dorado*, *An Area of Darkness*, *The Middle Passage*, *In a Free State* and *Guerrillas*, which was called by *The New York Times* "probably the best novel of 1975." A citizen of Britain, Naipaul lives with his wife in a flat in London.